Piece by Piece

DEBORAH WHITE

ISBN
979-8-89633-104-9 (Paperback)
979-8-89633-106-3 (eBook)

Page Solutions
541 Buttermilk Pike
Crescent Springs, KY 41017

Finally, a book on the Christian Life that is honest! Deborah does not hold back from sharing the details of her life—some sweet, but many filled with tremendous struggle. This book will take you on a journey to see how a faithful God continues to pursue His children. While there are no promises to an easy life, Deborah continues to point to the One who is in control of it all. Get ready to grapple first-hand with Genesis 50:20—man meant it for evil, but God meant it for good. Read and rejoice in a God who delights in rescuing and healing broken people. If you are wondering how to walk in your identity as a Christ-follower instead of being defined by your past, this book is for you!

Chris Brown, senior pastor, Southpoint Fellowship Church

"I have strength for all things in Christ Who empowers me." Philippians 4:13 (I am ready for anything and equal to anything through Him Who infuses inner strength into me; I am self-sufficient in Christ's sufficiency.) This verse describes Deborah. Her faith and strength in the Lord Jesus Christ have strengthened her. The unwarranted negative experiences, her struggles, and belief in some of the wrong people over the course of her life has made her strong, loving, and a caring lady. She has learned that things can get hard when she instantly wanted to do them independently without relying and leaning on the grace and mercy of God. As you read through her story, you will see God's grace and mercy, which was demonstrated by the Christlike people God put in her life. Through Deborah's mess she has emerged with a deeper faith in God. She has made her mess her message. Deborah has learned how great and deep God's love is for her.

I love you,

Dericka Deloney

As Deborah pours out her life story, we clearly see the effects of the fall through sinful people. Be prepared for your heart to ache on her behalf, but in the end, be prepared to give glory to the one True God "who raises the poor from the dust and lifts the needy from the ash heap to make them sit with nobles." Psalm 113:7-8 NASB

Blessings,

Kat Cogan

Having known Deborah since 1964 as seventh-grade classmates, I realize once again that God puts people in our path for a higher purpose. I am grateful I can remember her big, wide smile, her even bigger laughter, her beautiful tan complexion, her beautiful long, dark hair, her friendliness, and her fun-loving spirit. Little did I know and can hardly fathom the unimaginable pain behind this façade of beauty. I am grateful, all these years later, the Lord made our paths cross again, to give me a loving and caring friend who encourages me to look for the higher purpose in my life. She has overcome the worst childhood terror by knowing her true Savior. It is indeed my prayer that this book will show someone else with similar scars where true healing comes from. Thank you, Deborah, for showing me Jesus through your friendship, your humility, and your love for God.

Karen Robbins

Piece by Piece tells the amazing story of how God restored and sustained my dear friend Deborah through the ups and downs of life. Deborah is a living testimony of God's steadfast faithfulness and unwavering love. Though the difficult trials of life may seem to overwhelm, God is always walking with us as He restores our hearts—piece by piece.

Angie Stocker

It is such an honor to recommend this book, I believe that it will bring healing and awareness to so many people. Deborah is candid about what she has been through, because she has found forgiveness and healing that only comes through Jesus Christ. She and her sister Patricia are a testimony of what the Father can do in you when you truly forgive. I am blessed to call them my friends and sisters in Christ.

Linda Alexander

With candid clarity and courage, Deborah White reveals the traumatic and sometimes shocking abuses and challenges in her life along with her poignant determination to accept the forgiveness and healing that comes through Jesus Christ. Hers is a story of defeat transformed into victory, of feelings of shame and rejection turned into acceptance of God's pervasive love, of a life of complete turmoil that is remolded into one of joy and peace. Driven by the certainty that she could only find true wholeness through her faith and the recognition of what God has done in her life, Deborah learned to embrace God's steadfast faithfulness and unwavering love. Now, she wants to share with others- especially those with similar wounds- how true healing and complete wellness can be achieved.

"If you are wondering how to walk in your identity as a Christ-follower instead of being defined by your past, this book is for you! - Chris Brown, senior pastor, Southpoint Fellowship Church

Diane Eaton

I met Deborah White in a Bible study group in 2015. We became good friends and have shared lots of time in her home around a game table with other friends as well as various situations in public places. One of the first things I observed about her is that she seldom misses and opportunity to ask people she meets, "Do you know Jesus?"

I wish I had that kind of courage. After hearing her story, I think what gives her that drive is remembering where she came from, what God has done in her life, and wanting everyone to experience that kind of healing and wholeness that can only be found in Jesus.

She values the Word of God as her lifeline- which indeed it is for all believers. It has been, and continues to be, healing to her mind and heart

I pray Piece by Piece has motivated you to start or deepen a relationship with the Savior who loves you so much he wouldn't live without you.

Gloria Spencer

Contents

Dedication

This book is dedicated to:

- Christian White, my son, who, despite my many flaws, continues to convince me that I am a good mom. He consistently shows and provides encouragement and gives me unconditional love. No mother could be more joyful and proud. I love you.

- Rebecca, my friend, for giving me not just a place to live, but a place of refuge and strength in her heart and showing me the real true Jesus.

- Patricia Burgess, my twin sister, for being a part of my life. She has encouraged me along the way through her resilience, unconditional love, and continued validation. She has taken being a sister to a much higher level of being loved and adored. I love you.

- Debra Gentry, for the impact she's had on my life with her Biblical counseling, her teachings of spiritual truths, and her help toward my desired "progressive sanctification."

What a blessing she has been for me—as I am found in Him!

- Jesus Christ, for being my wellspring of hope! Whatever glory or hope comes from this book belongs exclusively to Him. He alone is worthy as I shall behold Him.

- And finally, I dedicate this book to our heavenly Father, King of Kings, Lord of Lords, who loved and pursued me from the very beginning to become His beloved daughter. I am so grateful and stand in complete awe of His amazing grace. I owe it all to YOU!

Acknowledgements

Thanks to:

- Sarah Tate, for her many hours of intense Christian counseling.

- Carla Wison, for her love and acceptance of me.

- Dr. Jenelle Martin, for her continued love and support that directed me the times I wanted to give up.

- My additional family, Molly and Clark, that offered me support and love as we weathered the storms set before us.

- Gloria Spencer, for transcription services and for helping with manuscript submission.

- Diane Eaton, a special thanks for taking this venture from manuscript to publication. You took the very heartfelt words off the pages to successfully capture my feelings, my pain, and desires to bringing the hope alive that I embrace only found in Jesus.

- And finally, to everyone who reads this book, who can identify with me the terrific heartache of one's pain. It is my complete, yearning desire that you, too, will answer the call of God to usher into your heart a change worth living.

Epigraph

O Lord, you have searched me and you know me.
You know when I sit and when I rise; you
perceive my thoughts from afar.
You discern my going out and my lying down;
you are familiar with all my ways.
Before a word is on my tongue you know it completely,
O Lord.
You hem me in—behind and before; You
have laid your hand upon me.
Such knowledge is to wonderful for
me, too lofty for me to attain.
Where can I go from your Spirit?
Where can I flee from your presence? If I
go up to the heavens, you are there;
if I make my bed in the depths, you are there.
If I rise on the wings of the dawn, if I settle on the far side
of the sea,
even there your hand will guide me, your
right hand will hold me fast.

If I say, "Surely the darkness will hide me and
the light become night around me,"
even the darkness will not be dark to you;
the night will shine like the day,
for darkness is as light to you.
For you created my inmost being;
you knit me together in my mother's womb.
I praise you because I am fearfully and wonderfully
made; your works are wonderful,
I know that full well.
My frame was not hidden from you when
I was made in the secret place.
When I was woven together in the depths of the
earth, your eyes saw my unformed body.
All the days ordained for me were written in
your book before one of them came to be.
How precious to me are your thoughts, O God!
How vast is the sum of them!
Were I to count them
they would outnumber the grains of sand.
When I awake, I am still with you.
If only you would slay the wicked, O God!
Away from me, you bloodthirsty men! They speak of you
with evil intent; your adversaries misuse your name.
Do I not hate those who hate you, O Lord, and
abhor those who rise up against you?

I have nothing but hatred for them; I count them my enemies. Search me, O God, and know my heart; test me and know my anxious thoughts. See if there is any offensive way in me, and lead me in the way everlasting.

Psalm 139 NIV

Foreword

On May 7, 2017, a letter arrived in my mailbox, and I immediately recognized Deborah's handwriting. She began by reintroducing herself, though I needed no such prompting to remember her vividly. I read the letter quickly since my eyes were drawn to the last paragraphs and the words she had underlined there: "You would be happy to know I am finally living the abundant life that Jesus talked about. Thanks to you, I finally have the peace of God within."

In addition to Deborah's powerful testimony contained in this book, we both give praise for God's faithfulness to work through frail human beings who are ready to be used by Him. This story unfolded as the Lord was pouring out His spirit in the Atlanta area. Many of us experienced this life-changing out-pouring and were seeking to understand the empowerment of the Holy Spirit—how to hear His voice.

When Deborah found herself without a place to live, the Holy Spirit spoke to my heart to open my home to her. My nest was empty, my two grown children had moved out on their own, and I had a spare bedroom available. And through all the upheaval that followed, the Holy Spirit continued to be my Counselor and Comforter, and Jesus, my Solid Rock.

Deborah lived in my home until she was ready to make a move on her own.

In my times with Deborah, I constantly pointed her back to Jesus as our only Hope and Salvation. Though the two of us lost contact when I moved to another city, the Holy Spirit continued to put her and her children in my mind for prayer. We can absolutely trust Him with our loved ones. He keeps His promises.

> "...being confident of this, that he who began a good work in you will carry it on to completion until the day of Christ Jesus."
>
> *Philippians 1:6 NIV*

Rebecca Hollingsworth

Preface

We are all products of our past environments, DNA, relationships, situations, and events. In this book, I want to share with you how, in my life, I was only able to find whole, complete wellness within the parameters of my faith in Jesus Christ, God my Father, and His Holy Spirit.

I consider my arduous journey of faith to be pure joy and I give all honor and gratefulness to God. In His grace, He kept pursuing me until I recognized His deep and faithful love for me. Jesus came gently after me with His love and then gave me a life worth living.

I pray that through reading this autobiography, God will enlighten your knowledge of His salvation through Jesus Christ and give you the zeal or hunger for a closer walk with Him. It is my utmost passion and cry from my heart that this book will point readers to the hope found only in Jesus Christ.

If you are searching for the truth in life, I pray with great anticipation that you will consume and digest the words in these pages as I tell you how Jesus is the only way. With complete frankness and sincerity, I pray you will choose, after full consideration, to freely accept Jesus Christ as your Lord, Master, and Savior. Let me share with you what God showed me, that through my personal hurts, grueling wounds, struggles, making many mistakes, and through the empowering spiritual truths on this journey, that He gave me a voice to be discovered. May you find your voice too as you listen to the desires that God put in your heart.

> *I pray that out of his glorious riches he may strengthen you with power through his Spirit in your inner being, so that Christ may dwell in your hearts through prayer. And I pray that you, being rooted and established in love, may have power, together with all saints, to grasp how wide and long and high and deep is the love of Christ, and to know this love that surpasses knowledge-that you may be filled to the measure of all the fullness of God.*
>
> *Ephesians 3:16-19 NIV*

God bless you as you walk toward your destiny of finding hope, transformation, and peace within.

Deborah White

Introduction

Music and songs have always reached inward into my hiding place with the Lord. For years, I would sing the words to songs as a prayer to God. Even when I didn't have the words, I would still sing the songs. To this day, I sing as my prayer to God.

I wrote these lyrics as a song from my heart and sang it to God. He has taken my pain and given me a song to sing:

YOU TOOK ME

You have rescued me from myself.
You have rescued me from every sin.
In your name there is peace.
In your name there is joy unspeakable.
You brought me out of the miry clay
From hence, giving me good days.
When my mother and father forsook me
You gave me hope, grace and love in you.
You took my heart
And made it anew, for you heard my every cry
When I could not go any further you came along with
open arms.
Today, you are my hope

Today, Lord, you love me
Today, I am your beloved
Today, I am yours.
Today Lord, you took all my sins and set me free.
Today, you gave me hope, for you are mine and I am yours.
Chorus
You, Lord, are my strength,
my salvation,
my keeper,
my high tower,
my shelter,
my refuge,
my deliverer,
my comfort,
my rock.
In you I put my trust.
In you I declare your goodness.
In you there is mercy.
In you there is grace.
In you there is love.
In you alone are my Lord of all Lords.
For you healed my broken heart
and bound my wounds and pain.
For you count the number of stars as call them all by name.
For great is my Lord and mighty in power.

* * *

Prologue

As I read this story, I wept. Every part of my sister's journey is the actuality and the reality; I have witnessed the events and trials she described. I have loved being her twin. We survived and endured all of this, and now we can give God the glory, exaltation, and power that we made it through.

When I was growing up, I wanted to be like Deborah and now I have witnessed within her the glory of God. I have seen such a remarkable change that God has done with her, and I watch her become a person I want to emulate.

Yes, I have often wondered why—why so much turmoil?—but God has led us all the way. He knew we could handle all the aspects of this journey and I give God the praise and honor that we came out on top. My sister and I have a special love for each other and toward God. God gave me a partner, my twin, to help me walk through the trials in my life and to become victorious in Jesus.

Sissy, all the years you talked to me about living for Jesus finally came to fruition in September 2014. Thank you for your continuous prayers before God that availed much on my behalf.

Sissy, besides God, you have been my rock, my tower of strength, and I love what God has done and is currently doing in our lives. He has taken our insecurities, fears, anxieties, and errors and has given us many victories and opportunities to learn about His amazing grace and undying love.

I love you.

Many blessings,
Patricia

* * *

When I read this book and think about my mom, I'm reminded of what Paul shared in his letter to the Ephesians: "For by grace you have been saved through faith. And this is not your own doing; it is the gift of God, not a result of works, so that no one may boast. For we are his workmanship, created in Christ Jesus for good works, which God prepared beforehand, that we should walk in them" (Ephesians 2:8-10 ESV).

As you read my mom's story, you will be confronted with the life of a girl. A girl that was overlooked, objectified, used, and left broken. This trend followed her into adulthood. To the world, Mom was tainted, she was used, and she had baggage. But I see her differently. God sees her differently. She is different. When I think about my mom, she is the perfect living example of what it means to be God's "workmanship." Over time she has stopped listening to the voices of people who want to get something from her and begun listening to the voice of God, who says that He wants to do something for her. I have seen up close the radical transformation of a broken, beat-down person, who has become a beautiful and vibrant daughter of God. I have seen her forgive when hatred seemed like the only option. I've seen her heal when brokenness seemed like a final state. I have seen her pray and trust, when everything around her seems like it's falling apart.

Mom, you are the strongest person I know. I love you. I respect you. I am honored to be your son. When I am confronted with my own brokenness, your testimony gives me hope. And I know it will also bring hope to the lives of the people who are blessed to read this book. Thank you for your submission to God. It's because of you that I believe in miracles.

I love you!

Christian White

* * *

1

In the Beginning

But he said to me,
"My grace is sufficient for you,
for my power is made perfect in weakness."
Therefore I will boast all the more gladly
about my weaknesses,
so that Christ's power may rest on me.
That is why, for Christ's sake,
I delight in weaknesses, in insults, in hardships,
in persecutions, in difficulties.
For when I am weak, then I am strong.

2 Corinthians 12:9-10 NIV

The great Christian apologist C.S. Lewis stated, "Pain is God's megaphone for calling you to Him." I believe that statement since pain—enduring pain—has called me to God Himself.

I am one of six children, born after my parents married each other for the second time.

I truly believe I was conceived because of a lustful action, not from a loving thought or a thought of being desired. My twin sister, Patricia, and I were born into an environment of anger and hatred.

Many years later, a few immediate family members admitted to us that, when Patricia and I were about three years old, my mother had beaten us so severely that we had been taken to the hospital and placed in an incubator packed with ice to recover from all the bruising. A doctor later confirmed the story when he reported to our adoptive parents that both of our heads showed signs of physical abuse.

My mother also told me much later that she had left my father two times due to his abuse of her. I wondered how she could have convinced herself that he would not inflict the same abuse on her children, too.

Soon after that beating, my parents separated and divorced a second time. Once my mother left the household, my father was left to raise all six of their children. I sensed that my father resented the fact that he got wedged into the situation of having to take care of us. We had altered his lifestyle, and as a result, we received harsh penalties every day for our wrong-doing. Many years later, my mother told me she left him due to his abusive nature toward her.

He later married a woman named Marilyn, and she became our stepmother. She had a son from her previous marriage. After only a few years of marriage, she and my father also divorced. Once again, we were left in the full and complete control of our father.

2

Abused

When you pass through the waters, I will be with you;
and when you pass through the rivers, they will not sweep
over you. When you walk through the fire, you will
not be burned; the flames will not set you ablaze.

Isaiah 43:2 NIV

Working a full-time job as a diesel mechanic and then coming home to raise six children had to be difficult for my dad. Still, tough as it may have been, it was even tougher on us. To discipline us, he used cruel and demeaning methods to get our attention. Worse, if one of us got into trouble, he would make us spank each other to make the message go further. Whoever was told to stand facing the other children, and the rest of us would have to line up to spank or hit the offender with a board. If you were one of the ones doing the hitting, and you failed to hit your sibling hard enough, my father would make all the others spank you as well. It was up to him to gauge how hard you were hitting, as we reluctantly tried to do what he said. When my twin and I were about six years old, we were forced to spend several days and nights standing in a small, dark closet without food. Separately. When I was in the closet, my father would come by and open the door to check on me. If he saw me kneeling from exhaustion, he would take me out of the closet, whip me with a belt or board, and dare me to kneel in the closet again.

Those days and nights spent in that tiny, darkened closet were agonizing and excruciating. We were without food, were not being able to go to the bathroom, and were not given anything to drink. There were many times when I would quietly sneak out of the closet to get an uncooked hot dog from the refrigerator to eat.

Patricia and I would try to hide food between the mattresses of our beds to eat later, still trying not to get caught by our father. We didn't care if the food was raw or that it had been stuck between the mattresses for days. Many years later, I found myself preferring to eat raw hotdogs to cooked ones.

Once, during a period when I was being cooped up in the closet for days on end, I ate part of my brother's freshly made birthday cake. My father noticed it was missing the following day and knew I had stolen the cake to eat, and he whipped me for it. Getting a beating for what he called stealing his food seemed better to me than being hungry for hours. I took the lesser of two evils to stave off my hunger and I undoubtedly paid the price for it.

Even at a young age, sexual abuse was a daily part of our lives. When my sister and I were in the bathtub together taking a bath, my Dad would regularly come into the bathroom, completely naked and grinning, and flaunt himself in front of

4

us. I'd keep my head down to avoid having to look at him. Even so young, I was too embarrassed and ashamed to look upon his nakedness.

A few years later, my father allowed my two oldest siblings—children from my parents' first marriage—to leave our home and go live with other relatives. At the venture of my mother's and father's second marriage to one another came another sibling that lived with my dad's friends. He relatively had it rough with his new set of parents and went back to live with our dad six years later. My dad was very physically and emotionally abusive toward my brother. A few years later my brother decided to leave and joined the Army to escape the abuse. As we connected many years forward, I learned that life was not easy for them either. Having parents that were abusive and utterly rejected us paved a hard road to walk obviously for all of us. But Patricia, my younger brother Richard, and I were left behind to continue to live with my father. As I look back, I have to admit that when all of my sisters and brothers lived together as a family, things were very chaotic for us. The three youngest of us—Patricia, my brother, and I—were a lot younger than our older siblings, and we witnessed a great deal of arguing and fighting between them. It was a very hostile environment. Then, one day, I woke up to find that my older siblings were not living at home anymore. No one explained it to us. And I instinctively knew not to question my dad.

Patricia and I slept beside one another in a pink bedroom which was just a few feet away from my father's bedroom. Inevitably, he would call out for one of us to come into his bedroom and share his bed. We had to take turns—first one, then the other—at regular, consistent intervals of time—for him to sexually molest us both.

As my father had his way with me, I was filled with shame, humiliation, disgrace, and embarrassment. But I kept them to myself, not wanting him to notice any changes in me. I was too frightened as to what he would do to me above and beyond the sexual abuse.

Five years later, as Patricia and I tried to help minimize each other's pain as much as possible. When it was my turn to go into our father's bedroom, I tried not to awaken her, hoping she could sleep as soundly as possible for as long as possible. I found out years later that she, too, did the same for me. We ached for one another while the other one was at the mercy of our father in his bedroom.

Sometimes I would try to protect my sister by crying out to my dad and telling him that I would stay with him longer if he didn't make my sister come to him. But it didn't make any difference. He wanted both of us.

The pain and embarrassment of what we were enduring made us insecure and emotionally devastated, and we would frequently wet the bed. And then we were punished for doing so. When my father discovered the telltale signs, he'd take both of us to the bathroom, fill the tub until it was almost full, and then kneel down by the tub with the two of us on either side of him. Alternating between the two of us, he would cup his big hands around one of our necks and, with a lot of anger and vigor, hold our heads underwater for a very long time. Then it would be the other's turn. He repeated the ritual at least eight to ten times each. I feared for my life, thinking I would be brought to my death each time my father performed this traumatic ordeal. I felt like I was drowning as I choked on the water going into my nose and mouth, fighting to breathe.

All the while, he would yell "This is for wetting the bed! This is for wetting the bed! Don't do it again!"

Then there were times when he would take things a step further. After dunking us in the tub, he'd raise the toilet seat and, taking us one after the other, angrily push our heads into the dirty toilet and flush it, screaming hateful remarks at us as he did so. I was humiliated beyond hope and feared that my hair and face were going to get flushed down the toilet.

Those episodes terrified me. Yet having to watch my dad physically abuse my sister made the ongoing hateful experience seven more devastating to endure.

Because of those occurrences, I developed a phobia of the bathroom and for most of my life, I've hated having to use the bathroom. I'd often hold in my urges until I absolutely could not wait any longer. As a result, I suffered severe stomach problems even into my adult years.

My twin sister and I lived in overwhelming fear and dread of my father. From one minute to the next, we never knew how he was going to treat us. We pretty much knew we were not being loved, but for some reason, we loved him and wanted to be near him anyway. Being abused and mishandled became our expected reality, but of course, we were young, and we didn't know that it was abuse. To us, it was what being raised as children looked like. We missed our older siblings but didn't want to be kicked out like they were. That's part of what kept us in check: we were afraid that if we did not obey him, then he would probably take steps to get rid of us, too, and we didn't want that. After each round of punishment, we made our apologies and promises to do better in the future so we could stay with him. I figured that I had to do my best to become a better child and win over his adoration and love. With everything I had, I tried to not make him angry, in the hopes that he would one day love me.

3

Leaving Home

*Though my father and mother forsake
me, the Lord will receive me.*

Psalm 27:10 NIV

My father's cruelty continued for eight long years. Over the course of those years, he continued his emotional, sexual, and physical abuse of my sister and me. With those conditions, intense feelings of shame became a part of my experience of who I was. I blamed myself for having to perform sexual acts that my dad demanded I perform. I knew deep within that it was inherently wrong, but at the same time, I thought it was normal, expected behavior from a father—anyone's father.

Just before we turned eight years old, on the final night that my sister and I spent under his roof, my father molested both of us once again. It lasted all night and all the next morning, and I still remember it vividly to this day. It was a dreadful and disgusting experience that continues to haunt me.

That next morning, the three of us got in the car to take a trip from our home in Texas to somewhere in Georgia. I wasn't sure where. Along the way, my father drove off the highway and wound his way up in front of a white house with shrubbery by the windows in the front yard. He instructed the two of us to get down and keep ourselves low by the floorboards of the car so we could not see or be seen.

I didn't follow his instructions. I looked out the window and realized that we had stopped at a house that, I found out later, was in Alabama. It was Mildred's—my biological mother's—house. My dad had stopped there to see if she wanted to take us in. It was a pointless request. She didn't want us. So, on to Georgia we went. It was December 11, 1959.

Years before, when my father was still married to Marilyn, the four of us had taken a trip to Arizona to visit Marilyn's parents. While we were there, my dad met a married couple that had no children of their own. They were related to my stepmother's family, so we visited them while we were in the area. The couple told my dad that if he ever decided that he wanted to let us go or get rid of us, they would take us in and become our parents. So, a few years later, that's exactly what he did. My dad tried to get rid of my sister and me and leave us with our mom. But she didn't want us.

After getting back on the road, my father stopped at someone else's home, a white house with a screened-in porch. A couple came to the door and after letting us in, treated us to a home-cooked meal. The three of us ate our supper there and spent the night. The next day, I looked out the window and saw that my dad had gotten in his car and driven off. He left my sister and me behind with two complete strangers without even saying goodbye.

4

New Parents

The Lord is a refuge for the oppressed, a
strong hold in times of trouble.
Those who know your name will trust in you, for you,
Lord, have never forsaken those who seek you.

Psalm 9:9-10 NIV

The strange couple told Patricia and me that we would be living with them from then on. They would become our "new parents." In private, I told my twin that they would never be my parents; I already had a mom and a dad. From the very start, I did not feel I belonged in that house with them. I deeply wanted my biological father's love and presence.

Life for the two of us would be very different at our new home. The first thing our adoptive parents did was cut off our long hair, which was very upsetting to us. But they did give us a lot of good food at each meal, which we had not been used to getting at our dad's house. At our very first Christmas there, they overwhelmed us with lots of gifts.

I was a very angry child at the time. In spite of the abuse and terror, I wanted my father to come back and get me. That's all I knew. I thought his behavior was normal. I did not know any better. Adjusting to the fact that I was being fed, clothed, and talked to in that first year with my new parents was quite challenging for me, in spite of some of the benefits. We did things and went places that we had not even come close to experiencing before, but I was too full of anger and fear to enjoy them.

In the meantime, our new "parents" spent a lot of time with us. Still, it was hard for us to adjust to our new environment; we had a very hard time in school academically and socially. But before long, we became popular at school, mostly because we were twins. At the same time, we were made fun of due to our dark skin tone. Even our adoptive parents were ashamed, uncomfortable, and embarrassed of our skin color and ethnicity. They told us not to play out in the sun because we could get tanned too quickly, and they didn't want us to get any darker than we already were. So, we only played outside after the sun went down. They also admonished us not to tell people that we were part Indian.

At some point, Patricia and I divulged to our new parents how our dad had treated us, abused us, and used us sexually. We pleaded with them not to hurt us in any of the ways he had— sexually, physically, or emotionally. We were terribly ashamed and embarrassed to have to tell them about all of it, but we couldn't pretend anymore that it hadn't happened. And we needed to try to make sure that the terror wouldn't happen again. They both promised us they would never do anything remotely close to what my father had done and assured us it was the last abuse we would experience.

They didn't quite keep their promise. Angry as we were, con-fused and hurt as we were, we would often get into trouble, and trouble led to harsh punishment. We were often spanked with a belt and we were threatened with being taken back to our dad if we didn't do this or that just right. They also frequently tried to tell us that our birth mother was a prostitute, that she was no good, and that she didn't want us. They would tell us that our mother did not love us and that if we didn't stop getting into trouble, they would put us in a convent. Now, my sister and I had attended a Catholic school when we had been living with our father. We had a lot of bad experiences there. There had been many times that my hands had been bruised from the numerous strikes of a ruler, administered by a nun for misbehaving at school. So, we knew for sure we did not want to go back there and receive mistreatment there too. The threat of living in a convent really scared us.

In fact, it was constantly used as a threat to control us and keep us in line. Once again, we were being emotionally abused. That, and repeatedly being told that our biological parents didn't love us and that they didn't deserve to be parents.

Because of these accusations, my sister and I took the blame that we were the reason our biological parents didn't love or want us. We were responsible for our parents' abandonment and lack of love. We were never told anything different.

5

Camp Meetings

*You hear, O Lord, the desire of the afflicted; you
encourage them, and you listen to their cry, defending
the fatherless and the oppressed, in order that man,
who is of the earth, may terrify no more.*

Psalm 10:17-18 NIV

When my sister and I were nine years old, our adoptive
mother started taking us to "camp meetings" in the summers. It
was a ten-day camp that preached and taught people about Jesus
Christ, and it became a highlight of my childhood. My mother
owned a three-room cottage on the grounds. The attendees
were from all over the U.S. and came to stay and listen to the
sermons. We stayed in dorms, cottages, and motel rooms and
dined and played together, went swimming and played ping
pong. Since our parents had bought us a ping pong table for
Christmas one year, I was completely determined to win every
game I could. I learned to put a curve on my serve as a method

of winning games. To this day, I have friends from "camp meeting" whom I cherish.

Frankly, we were not being raised to have a relationship with God or Jesus. We were raised to be focused on the "do's" and "don'ts" and rules. But it was at camp meeting that I heard about repentance. I knew I didn't want to be bad, and I didn't want to go to a bad place called Hell.

So, at the age of nine, I started hearing about Jesus, about going down to the altar, about repenting, and about asking Jesus into my heart. I was completely earnest and honest with this Jesus and wanted him to come inside my heart to love me. Even at that young age, I would often hear the voice of God beckoning me as He would draw me closer to finding out about Him.

But once camp was over, those "good" feelings would only last about a month before I would begin to feel and act badly all over again. When I looked at people, all I saw was that they didn't love me. I was too scared to trust anyone. I lived in fear and in complete apprehension as I felt unloved and unwanted. It was a ferocious battle of the mind for me.

I heard from both my biological and my adoptive parents that I was unworthy of their love. My relationships with everyone suffered, to say the least. I did not know how to cope with all those mixed feelings. I think it was my anger that kept me afloat.

Not surprisingly, I suffered from depression, too, and I didn't receive any treatment for it. Counseling was not offered to children in those days as readily as it is now. Patricia and I bottled up all of our hurt, rejection, and confusion inside. Only the anger showed on the outside.

My adopted parents took up the practice of disciplining us by whipping us. Many times, I refused to cry while being whipped with a thick leather belt; as a result, I got whipped more times and harder. If I cried, I got beaten. If I didn't cry, I got it worse. It was a no-win situation.

Here's how it went down. Generally, my mother would wait for my father to come home to administer the spankings. All the bedroom doors were closed, and the attic fan was turned on to obscure any loud noises. We were told to stand in the hallway with our arms down beside our legs while a belt was used against us. Meanwhile, the other twin would often have to stand by and watch and wait while the first one got whipped, all the while, feeling the hurt of the other.

Acting in defense of the other sister would only increase the punishment.

The other form of punishment my adopted mother used was to make us learn scriptures from the Bible—the Beatitudes, the Lord's Prayer, the books of the Bible, the 23rd Psalm, and other verses. I wasn't too fond of God or the Bible at that time. Learning scriptures was a long process, and that meant that the offense was drawn out longer due to my troubles with memorization.

We also had to write sentences on paper over and over again, sometimes thousands of times, over and over. I often got this punishment because I had run off with my mouth. We had to number the sentences we wrote and were given a time limit to have them done or the number would be doubled. The longer it went on, the worse it got.

6

Abused Again

Surely it was for my benefit that I suffered such anguish.
In your love you kept me from the pit of destruction;
You have put all my sins behind your back.

Isaiah 38:17 NIV

In November 1963, after John Kennedy's death, my new father sexually molested me. I was twelve years old. I had developed asthma and bronchitis and was very sick. He told my mother and me that he needed to sleep with me to take care of me. I kept turning away from him, pretending to be asleep, hoping he would restrain himself, but he continued the whole night and into the morning. My mind was racing with fear, and I felt dirty and shameful. Plus, he had betrayed our trust, so I was confused and hurt at the same time.

The next morning, my first thought was that he had given me his word that he would not sexually abuse either one of us. I felt my world was coming to an end. I was thoroughly disheartened, confused, hurt, and scared.

I had become a little girl filled with even more anger. I didn't trust anyone, and it showed. So, because of my attitude, two years later, our adoptive parents drove us to visit our real dad who was living in Arizona. Traveling for several days in a car, being so angry, and not knowing where we were going was very hard on me. I hated being in a car for such a long time with my parents. My mother kept asking me to apologize to my father at each stop, but I refused. When we finally arrived at my real dad's house, I was thrilled to see him.

Our adoptive parents told my dad—right in front of my twin and me—that they no longer wanted us as their children. My sister and I weren't surprised. On many occasions, they had told us that if we didn't behave, they would take us back to the parents that did not love nor want us. Now they were doing it.

It seemed like great news to me!

But, seeing us for the first time in six years, my dad sat me on one side of his lap and my sister on the other. Then he told us that he didn't love us and that we were the cause of his divorce. He told us that we would have to return to Georgia to live with our adoptive parents. I couldn't cry. I just felt shocked and empty inside. Our adoptive parents sat there gleaming as if they had just won the lottery.

I didn't realize it then, but that trip was just another way they came up with trying to control my actions. They continuously pointed out that they were "great" people that had rescued us from abandonment and rejection from our parents.

Two days later, we left Arizona and went back to Georgia. I felt like a Mac truck had just run over me. I was so disheartened and kept it secret and quiet inside of my head.

Again, and again over the years, until I turned the age of 18, my sister and I were whipped all the while being reminded that our biological dad and mom didn't love us or want us. Anger and hurt feelings encompassed my life. I felt totally unworthy of love. I was so hurt to continually hear those negative things about my biological parents from my adopted parents and confused about how my adoptive parents did not want us or love us either.

Once when I was 14, I took my mother's gun, pointed it at her head and asked her if she wanted to be shot. Then I turned and threw the gun down and fled out of the house. I came home later that same day, afraid I would be in big trouble, but I did not suffer any consequences from it.

Our house had a window in the bathroom I shared with my sister. The clear window was located at the very top of the wall. My sister and I would often be in the bathroom together, one taking a bath while the other used the lavatory or toilet. I looked up toward the window and saw our adoptive father's face staring down at us. His face was also reflected in the mirror as he watched us bathing and getting dressed. Later, I realized that he had to climb on top of his toilet to be able to look through that window. He did that many times, but we never said anything to him about it. We were both too scared to say anything, thinking it would result in us being thrown out with no place to go at all.

7

Adoption

When the set time had fully come, God sent his Son…
that we might receive adoption to sonship.

Romans 4:4-5 NIV

As a child, the idea of being adopted brought me a lot of pain. Other children ridiculed both me and my sister about it. And of course, our adoptive parents continually reminded us that our biological parents really didn't love us. Later, we realized that the kids who were ridiculing us must have learned their attitude from their own parents. My adoptive mother taught school, so she is probably the reason that word got out that we were adopted.

Although we moved in with our new parents when we were eight years old, they didn't legally adopt us until we were 18. They only told us it was going to happen a few days before the day that the adoption took place, and we were very disheartened about the news.

Privately, we knew it was the last day we would be considered the children of our biological parents. In a deep sense, children always want to be with their own parents, even if they are being abused. Abuse has a way of hiding a child's love and desire to be with their own parents. During the meeting with both sets of our parents and their attorneys, my sister and I were both sad and reluctant to sign the paperwork that would finalize our adoption, but we did so anyway.

Our new parents even tried to change our date of birth to the date when they got us and tried to change the city and state of our birth as well. We told the attorney we wanted everything to stay exactly as it was originally. We had already been told a lie about being officially adopted and we felt if they changed any other information, that would be a lie, too. The thought of being superficially incorrect with any detail of our birth seemed wrong.

Again, feelings of shame and not being good enough overtook me. Being adopted filled me with grief. It was far from a feeling of being chosen; it was a feeling of being inferior. Sitting in the attorney's office, both of us cried—but we did so quietly, because our adopted parents were in the next room. Fast forward to about forty years later, the church I was attending offered a class about knowing God on a deeper level. In that class, they talked about how God sees us as His adopted sons and daughters. After all those years, I was still having a hard time with the idea of being adopted. It was not pleasant for me at all, so I walked out of the class. I couldn't handle it.

It reminded me of two people who didn't have any children of their own and really did not want them. I was afraid that God would look at me the same way my adoptive parents did—as someone else's rejected or unwanted child.

Upon hearing the term "adoption," I started wondering if God was forced to like me. I thought maybe He didn't do so willingly. Typically, people think of God in a similar way to how they perceive their parents and relate it to how they were treated or mistreated. So, the feeling of being adopted by God was not high on my list.

Several years later, I found myself sitting through a sermon about being adopted. The scripture text was Ephesians 1:5, which states that He predestined us for adoption to sonship through Jesus Christ, in accordance with His pleasure and will. My heart waged a huge tug-of-war about the good news. But the key word for me was "predestined." It was predetermined or foreordained that I would be His daughter. That helped calm the war within me.

Thankfully, I have since learned to welcome the idea of being chosen. Being chosen to belong to His family is my vision of truth. God knew the right time and the right place for me to receive that perception, for therein lies the paradigm shift to the joyful and peaceful attitude He wanted for me.

8

Boarding School

*At one time we too were foolish, disobedient, deceived
and enslaved by all kinds of passions and pleasures… But
when the kindness and love of God our Savior appeared,
he saved us, not because of righteous things we had
done, but because of his mercy.*

Titus 3:3-5 NIV

During camp meeting one summer, my sister had met a
boy who was talking about going to a private boarding school
in Rabun Gap, Georgia. So, the next school term, our parents
allowed her to go to Rabun Gap and attend the same school.
But once she was gone, I began to miss her terribly. It was
the first time we had ever been apart. So, three weeks later, at
my request, they sent me to join her. It was such a relief to be
away from home. I finally felt free from being subject to their
restraints and abuse.

But after a while, I decided to transfer to another boarding school, which was located in Toccoa Falls, Georgia. The years I spent there in Toccoa Falls Academy were the best years of my young adult life. I was able to take out a lot of my anger by playing sports. I was a good cheerleader and tennis player and I did well in basketball, scoring 40+ points at each game. I even received an MVP award in basketball in my senior year.

At Christmas, my biological brother called my adoptive parents to see if he could come get my twin and me to visit him in Mobile, Alabama. It had been at least 12 years since we had seen each other. My parents agreed.

By that time, my sister and I had only heard terrible things about our biological mother, but my brother brought up the idea of visiting her. With all that we had heard about her and her irresponsible behavior, we were hesitant to go see her. But my brother felt very strongly about it and insisted that we go. After all, we hadn't seen her since we were three years old.

When we arrived at my mother's sister's home, we realized that they were having some sort of a party. When we walked in, my mother and her sister were sitting in the front room with some drinks in their hands, and they immediately started laughing at my twin and me. We weren't used to being around drinkers, so we didn't drink with them. My mother started saying mean things to us, including the fact that she didn't like that we were raised in a non-alcoholic environment.

She and her sister accused us of thinking that we were better than everyone else. The truth was, of course, that we felt very insecure and uncomfortable. She told everyone that we carried a Bible in our back pocket, and let it be known that she thought that we needed to let loose and have some fun. After spending just a short time with her, we were more confused and hurt about our relationship with her than ever.

After returning home, my adoptive father told me that he knew we had gone to see our mother, and he was furious with us. To get revenge, he told us that he would no longer pay for my boarding school fees and that I could go live with her. I told him we were forced into seeing her, but it didn't make any difference to him. He didn't care.

I knew my mother didn't want me and I couldn't go live with her. Fortunately, the school came to my rescue and allowed me to live on campus with my basketball coach and his wife.

In May of 1970, I graduated from high school. It had been a wonderful time for me. I was popular with my classmates and had received some validation as a person while I was there. I had excelled in sports and had been free of any kind of sexual exploitation or emotional or verbal abuse. So far, it was the best few years of my life.

9

Abuse Exposed

The Lord is gracious and righteous; our God is full of compassion.
The Lord protects the unwary; when I
was brought low, he saved me.

Psalm 116:5-6 NIV

It wasn't until my twin and I were almost 20 years old that anyone knew that our adoptive father had molested both of us.

When I was planning to be married in December 1971, I let the cat out of the bag and told the long story of his abuse of me to my sister. Then she told me what he did to her. So, I told our adoptive mother about it.

Her reaction was to tell me that a rat had done it, not her husband. While I had been living with deep shame and embarrassment, our adoptive mother didn't believe that the offense had ever occurred. She was so angry, she made us go stay in a hotel room, and we didn't know what would happen to us. We thought we were going to be given up or taken to live elsewhere. Again, we felt our safety and lifestyle were in jeopardy. Yet again, we felt unwanted, unbelieved, and unloved. A month later, my adoptive father died of a heart attack. His brothers and sisters collectively blamed me for his death, and, to this day, they refuse to have anything to do with me. They shamed my sister and me for telling the truth about this man.

10

Love and Marriage

*Better a patient person than a warrior, one with
self-control than one who takes a city.*

Proverbs 16:32 NIV

I started my very first job when I was 20 years old, and
that was where I met my future husband. We dated for a short
while and then married. I didn't have the first clue how to act or
treat someone, much less have the social skills to even consider
getting married. Nightmares of my past haunted me, and I
kept hearing the voices inside of my head as to how "no good"
I was. Battle scars from my childhood plagued my marriage and
every other relationship I had. I was plagued with extreme anger
within myself and with others. As a result, I was frequently
emotionally unstable and confused and would have emotional
outbursts. Even though I told him about all the abuse I suffered,
after we were married, he never really knew he would be coming
home to. Even while we dated, our time together was full of

conflict and contentious, and of course it got even worse once we were married.

I was often unfaithful. I kept looking to be loved. My husband knew I had been adulterous. All I found through those experiences was more shame and guilt. My marriage was one big struggle after another.

I gave birth to four children. One died before childbirth and the other three suffered from being born to a mother who was irate much of the time. Not surprisingly, they showed evidence of confusion and hurt due to my instability and volatility.

To hide my pain, I turned to drugs, alcohol and sex. Spiritually, I was on a rollercoaster—up and down. When I was on the uphill climb, I had some relief emotionally. When I started spiraling downward, I hated and distrusted God. I was so angry with him.

11

Fists to God

Like a city whose walls are broken through
is a person who lacks self-control.

Proverbs 25:28 NIV

I remember telling God I thought He was egotistical and terribly selfish. With my tainted, corrupted perception of God I thought he was self-seeking and self-centered for wanting to be worshipped. So I went about cursing God, using all the profanity I knew, and I'd dare Him to come down from heaven to meet me one-on-one. With all the anger I was holding inside me, I would literally point my finger upward and tell Him how I would beat him up using my hands if He came down, since He was obviously too scared to come near me. And I really thought I could do it.

I couldn't understand how He could protect and love other people, but not me. Thinking about it brought feelings of unworthiness and lack of trust, which led me to reject God.

I also feared that God Himself might abuse me along with all the others. I figured I was only created to be abused. Period. It was the only way I could make sense of everything that had happened.

I kept hearing Satan say to me, "Your own parents didn't want you, so why would God want you?" I hadn't yet learned that the scripture then says that if your mother and father forsake you, the Lord will pick you up. (Psalm 27:10 NIV)

Every year at camp meeting, I literally cried out for God to love me and want me. At those times, I noticed the emptiness—the void—within me being filled with God coming after me. Often, I even felt the wooing of God calling me out. I heard a small, still voice saying that He loved me. But I didn't trust that either.

Trying to be a Christian, I messed up repeatedly. I just could not get it right. I continuously hit rock bottom. I couldn't perform with this Jesus inside my heart. Many different feelings, especially feelings of unworthiness and shame, defined my character and attitude.

I remember feeling as though I was in my own private prison, feeling handcuffed with the fetters of captivity. I felt chained in "unbelief," encumbered with fear, restrained with doubts and worries, gripped ferociously with repressed anger, confined with the certainty of being faithless, shackled by confusion, hampered with anxiety, and, last but not least, bound spiritually with a deep, sinking feeling. Having these manacles vastly limited my sensitivity and assessment of God's competence to want me. I could not fathom God desiring to love me.

Having my last child at age thirty-eight was extremely hard on me physically and emotionally. I remember vividly being very depressed following her birth and was not being treated for it. When my daughter was three months old, and my sons were two and twelve, I was in a bad way with my marriage, confused and hurt and feeling bad about myself. I decided to do the best thing, the right thing, for me and for my children. I moved out of the house into a new environment.

Soon after that, I did what I had done before. With my fist pointed upwards towards the heavenly realms, I screamed at God. "God, if you think you're so big, come down here, and I will kick your butt. You don't want any part of me. I'll get you!"

Somehow, I felt like I had to tell Him off before He could tell me what a disappointment and failure that I had been.

Yet amid all my pain, God kept pursuing me. He would send the right person at the right time, telling me how much He loved me. But the more He pursued me, the angrier I became.

I continued to pull back from God. I deliberately wanted to do the things I knew that would make Him even madder at me. I knew and saw that people were easily repelled by me if I made them mad, so why not God? Realistically, my life and feelings were totally reactive toward God as to how people treated or mistreated me. I thought that if people hated me, then God would surely hate me. I had no earthly clue that He was a pure, truthful, and loving God.

My mind couldn't grasp that God could actually love me. Yet I kept hearing a small, quiet voice that God did indeed love me. Even so, I had taught myself not to trust what I heard inside of my head.

12

Pamela

He who dwells in the shelter of the Most High
will rest in the shadow of the Almighty.

Psalm 91:1 NIV

After 22 years of marriage, my husband wanted a divorce. I was a total wreck. While I had known a divorce was inevitable I felt betrayed. A marriage without Jesus running it was doomed from the very beginning. Before I got the news about the divorce, I met Pamela, a woman who lived in the same town I lived in. She wanted to talk to me about God. She invited me to her home and then let me pour out all my feelings about my husband having an affair. She pointed me toward Jesus and told me He would help me.

I was deeply depressed. I didn't have a clue who I was. I wanted my life to end. The impact of a failed relationship with my husband felt like it too much for me to bear. I felt like I had virtually no support and I started having repeated suicidal thoughts, which would continue for years to come. Thoughts of destruction bombarded me with feelings of discouragement, anger, fear, and remorse. I felt overwhelmed with sadness, distress, and bewilderment. I felt lost and apprehensive. The thought of getting a divorce and living in the unknown was extremely frightening to me. My feelings of being abandoned, discarded, worthless and neglected where all triggered and intensified.

A month later, I moved in with Pamela and her family. Everywhere Pamela went, I was right there by her side— shopping, at the grocery store, everywhere. Pamela went to a Charismatic church; it was something I had never experienced before. I had never seen people raise their hands and shout praises to God. It was a totally different environment. I had never seen people praising God in that way. I had only been taught to worship God by singing a hymn—there was no expression of joy or thankfulness in it.

Pamela and her close friend, Rebecca, had a joy in them that I had never seen. They talked about their relationship with God and having a kind of love for Him that I didn't know about. Over time, they showed me a love and acceptance I'd never known before.

Regardless of their love and care for me, I had more hurt in my heart than I could deal with. My thoughts of suicide were tormenting me. One day, I went to a local store and bought a gun and ammunition. But after I got back in my car and passed a lake by the side of the street, I stopped my car, got out, and threw the gun into the lake. I still wanted to end my life but there was something different about those two women that made me want their God.

13

Joyce Meyer

Therefore, if anyone is in Christ, he is a new creation; the old has gone, the new has come.

2 Corinthians 5:17 NIV

About six months later, I went to a Christian biblical retreat at Callaway Resort & Gardens in Pine Mountain, Georgia. Joyce Meyer, a Christian speaker that I had seen on TV, was going to be speaking at the retreat. I knew very little about Joyce Meyer, but I had heard she had been sexually abused by her father, as I had been. Her talk was inspiring, and after she was done, we were told that anyone could go into an office with her in the back and she would pray with them. So I stood in line to wait my turn.

When I met with her, Joyce told me that God told her I had a past like hers and that God was going to heal me.

The idea that God could talk to people was completely new to me, but He surely did that evening. I was amazed to hear her tell me things that she couldn't have known any other way. To this day, I still listen to Joyce Meyer as she talks about God's redeeming power to love and to restore those that submit to Him.

A year later, I saw Joyce speak again, this time in Atlanta. Once again, people were invited to go to a back room and pray with her. She came to me again and touched my shoulder and I got what charismatic Christians call "slain in the Spirit."

I had secretly prayed to God to let that experience take place within me. I wanted to know if God was really behind such an experience because I didn't trust people; I thought maybe they were just faking it. I thought they might be willingly falling to the ground to get attention or to make people think they were having some important experience with God.

But then it happened to me. The only thing I remember is hearing Joyce pray and then being awakened, finding myself on the floor and needing to stand up. I had completely passed out for a few minutes.

Over the years of knowing her, Joyce Meyer has made a believer out of me. She has always been consistent in her teachings about God's love. I have read many of her books and heard many of her talks. Her life has been very significant for me in pursuing my life in Jesus. I know she knew the pain I was living in. She, with a strong conviction to honoring God, completely understands how He intervenes with His grace into broken, frag-mented lives. She has been very instrumental in transforming my life as she points out that God loves and heals the hurting, shattered ones.

14

Love & Manipulation

Jesus answered,
"I am the way and the truth and the life.
No one comes to the Father except through me."

John 14:6 NIV

Even as I was searching to find out who God is, I fell into more tragic circumstances. A "Christian" person befriended me, and I began to trust her—something that was hard for me to do. With hesitation, I shared with her my secrets and details of my early childhood abuse and failed marriage. I felt comforted by her words that God wanted to heal my hurts. With an insistent firmness, she told me that God Himself wanted to love me— and that His love would be shown through her.

I did not have a clue what that meant. So I told her to "bring it on." As I began to reveal to her many of the truths of my life, she learned quickly that I had never felt that I was loved. She told me that that would change. She repeated the idea that

Christian people would love me through God. I did not know what to expect; I wholeheartedly wanted to open myself to this newfound love from God and His people.

By sharing with this woman about my father's sexual abuse, I began to feel an undeniable trust and sense of peace. I felt comforted. Sharing my pain gave me the acceptance I yearned for, and I did not feel so shameful allowing her into the depths of my heart and soul.

As time passed, and I talked honestly about the sexual abuse, I began to gain a new perspective about my past. She kept telling me that God loves me so—a message that I had been desperate to hear for many, many years. She insisted that I was "special" in God's eyes. I started to trust her.

Then it all turned horribly wrong.

Out of nowhere, the woman started to make sexual advances towards me. I was confused. I tried to ask her what it was all about. But in response to my questions, she only insisted, "How dare you question me and not hear the voice of God to accept this!" She said that I had been specifically appointed to be loved by Him—through her. She claimed that she had a special mission to give me something I have never had—love. It was a gift from God, she said.

My daily visits turned sexual in nature and I struggled with what I was doing with her. I searched for the truth but got no answers. I knew I did not hear the voice of God, so why should I question the validity of the experience? I knew that practicing that kind of lifestyle is wrong to God. But the emphasis was spelled out to me that I did not hear from God and that she did. I hated what I was doing but I felt trapped since I wanted to be loved so desperately. I was so hungry to feel love and acceptance. Feelings of confusion were woven with shame and betrayal as if I was that same little girl being molested all over again. I felt resistant and angry about being "loved" by God through this "Christian" woman.

I was completely confused.

15

Suicidal

The fear of man will prove to be a snare, but
whoever trusts in the Lord is kept safe.

Proverbs 29:25 NIV

In 1990, just after Christmas, Pamela and I had a falling out. So she asked me to move out of her home, and I moved in with Rebecca.

After seeing how I was handling things, Pamela decided that I needed some deep spiritual cleansing. Both Rebecca and Pamela started to take me to a "deliverance minister" on a weekly basis. In Christianity, deliverance ministry is called on to cleanse a person of evil spirits and demons in order to address the problems that are arising within their life.

During my sessions, I talked with two ministers while Pamela and Rebecca waited in another room. Before I told the ministers about my recent experience with the "Christian" woman, I asked both of them to promise me that they would not tell a soul what I was about to tell them. They both agreed. So, I told the two ministers about my sexual encounter with the woman I'd been seeing, and I told them how she kept insisting that God was purposely and deliberately involved. I told them how confused I was with what had emerged between the two of us.

After the session, the ministers met with Pamela and Rebecca. Later, as the three of us drove home, Pamela got upset. She asked me what was going on with me—and with whom—sexually. They insisted that I tell them the whole story, so I relented. They told me that the deliverance ministers were going to report what had happened, even after they had agreed not to.

As soon as we got to Rebecca's house, I went upstairs to my room and closed the door. Once again, I felt thoroughly betrayed by Christianity. I was done and tired of it all. So, I swallowed 300 aspirins, thinking that would kill me.

When Rebecca came to the door to check on me, I yelled out that I wanted to kill myself and I had just taken 300 aspirin. She called the police, of course, and they sent an ambulance.

At the hospital, the nurses pumped my stomach. Then I was sent to a mental hospital ward for trying to end my life. Visitors who came to see me told me they didn't blame me for what had happened; they agreed that I had been taken advantage of.

I was released from the mental facility two weeks later yet feeling abused and betrayed once again. Adding to the trauma, Pamela and Rebecca were told that the two of them would no longer be accepted in the church they were presently attending if they continued to help me. Thankfully, they decided to stand by me and left the church.

I found out later that nothing had been done to rectify what the Christian woman had done to me. I got into trouble because I told the truth, and then I was told I could never show up there again to worship. It was just like what happened when I was a little girl: I told the truth about what my adopted father did to me, but I got the blame and the shame.

16

Court

The Lord will fight for you; you need only to be still.

Exodus 14:14 NIV

For many years after that incident, I continued to be tormented by wanting to end my life. Thoughts of being pushed out and of not being wanted clouded my perspective of God. I had a big chip on my shoulder against God and people that called themselves Christians.

The experience left me feeling completely bruised and confused—emotionally and spiritually. I was determined to avoid any type of relationship, especially with anyone who said they had God in their heart. I had many questions for God; I was left disheartened and discouraged.

In 1994, I had to appear in court for divorce proceedings from my husband. Until that time, the children had been living with their father except for a few overnight stays with me and frequent daytime activities. I was hoping to get custody of them, so I could be a full-time mother again.

Sitting in the courtroom were several people who were there to speak to the judge against me. Even a therapist I had been seeing was there for my husband's case. She was there to tell the court that I wanted to kill my husband. I remembered the session. She asked me how I felt about him cheating with my close relative.

"Didn't you just feel like killing him?" she asked me. "Yeah. I wish he was dead," I replied in response.

My attorney decided to settle out of court, so no witnesses were called to testify after all. With that, the judge decided to have my children stay with their father until July 15 of the following year. I was so heartbroken at the news that I wailed and cried out loud. Even though I would be allowed to see them on weekends, I thought my opportunity to be a full-time mother was over.

But when July 15th finally arrived, my children moved with me into a new little home I had purchased.

17

Fall

*Even though I walk through the valley of the shadow
of death, I will fear no evil, for you are with me;
your rod and your staff, they comfort me.*

Psalm 23:4 NIV

On October 29, 1994, the children and I visited my twin sister
at her home. She had several horses, and we all decided to go
horseback riding together. My daughter sat with me on one of
the horses and we started off having a lovely day. Two weeks
later, I woke up from a coma.

I was told that I had fallen off the horse onto asphalt and
had hit my head twice, which put me into a coma. I had been
badly hurt, my brain was swollen, and I had a broken collarbone
and other injuries. My head was so swollen from the internal
bleeding that it was as big as a basketball, according to my
sister. It was an acute subdural hematoma, which, when due to
trauma, is the most lethal of all head injuries and has a high

46

mortality rate if it is not treated immediately with surgical decompression. To relieve the swelling on my brain, the doctors planned to drill holes in my head, but just before the procedure began, blood started gushing out of my ears, nose, and mouth, so it was no longer necessary.

They told my children that I only had a 50/50 chance of survival.

The fall had knocked everything out of me. I had to relearn everything—how to talk, how to walk, how to say the alphabet, how to add and subtract. Everything. My speech was impaired, and I could not grasp or understand what people were saying if they talked a little too fast. My ability to comprehend words was deeply impaired.

Later, my Jewish doctor told me that I had kept trying to lead him to Jesus. I remember hearing from Satan, telling me the accident was God's fault—that God was trying to kill me. Satan kept telling that God wanted me dead, and that was the thanks I got for trying to serve Him.

Meanwhile, I also heard from God. He spoke to me clearly and told me He wanted me to remember Romans 8:29. He said he gave Romans 8:28 for many people: "All things work together for good to those who love God, who are called according to His purpose." But He also said that I needed to take in verse 29 as well: "For those whom He foreknew, He also predestined to become conformed to the image of His Son, so that He would be the firstborn among many brethren."

Over the years, He has inscribed that verse on my heart and mind as He predetermined me to becoming more like Jesus.

At Christmastime, I came home, but I was still unstable and was having trouble dealing with the reality of my circumstances. I was told by Satan that I was no good for my children, and I agreed. Several times I tried to take my life, overdosing on pills. I could not bathe myself; I had to be spoon-fed. During those horrible times, my children also suffered with depression and worry. My mind could not grasp the complexity I caused for them. I wholeheartedly believed that they needed me to go away.

One day, out of the blue, I decided to call my biological mother. When she picked up the phone, I told her that I had suffered a head injury, and I asked her if she could come to help. I thought it might be a good time to get to know my real mother, after all, and I figured that it would be a time that she could spend with her grandchildren too. She responded by telling me that she was sorry she had given birth to me. She told me never to call her again. I was devastated. For many years to come, her words rang in my ears.

Though my own mother did not care about me, the people at the church I was attending did. They helped me in many ways, from cooking and preparing meals for me, to just extending kindness. One precious friend bought Christmas presents for my children that year. Another came over to my house, gave me baths, and cleaned the house on many occasions. Others helped me by driving me to see the doctor, going with me to buy groceries, and running errands for me when needed.

Then my ex-husband took me back to court. He was claiming that I was unfit to be a full-time parent. The judge told us we needed to settle it between ourselves. I had been keeping a journal of all that I did to take care of my children, even when I was incapable of doing anything else, and I showed it to him. Because of that, he decided to let me keep the children on a full-time basis as their custodian parent.

What I was going through was taking a toll on me. My frontal lobe—the part of the brain that controls important cognitive skills such as emotional expression, problem solving, memory, language, judgement, and sexual behavior—had been damaged. It is the "control panel" of one's personality and one's ability to communicate. I had to learn how to live life in every way all over again. I had to relearn my relationship with God. I suffered both long-term and short-term memory loss. I was dependent on people pretty severely, and I was emotionally all over the place. For four years, I could not drive a vehicle.

Despite all of it, I can honestly say I believe I am better off for having had that experience. It took years for me to become a stable, rational, balanced person again. But I did.

During the process, I would get hope from the Bible. From that point onward I made better decisions, but it took time.

I am sure those years took a tremendous toll on my children as well. Yet they were very loving and patient with me during those rough times. I was learning my ABC's while my youngest child was learning hers. I spent as much time with my children as I could, as the two youngest were both in school and played sports. They managed better than I did and were very helpful to me. I just wanted to be a very loving mother and provide a stable home life for them.

Living through a traumatic brain injury was problematic for all of us. Every time I saw a doctor, they'd shake their head and say how well I was doing. I was doing much better than expected; I had been given a prognosis that claimed I'd never be able to regain stability or clear thinking, yet I seemed to be getting better and better.

But God! God patiently revived and healed me, and I give Him the praise and glory! Though I didn't recognize it at the time, He was right there with me. Looking back, I am amazed as to what He has done in my life.

18

Sunday School

*May our Lord Jesus Christ himself and God our
Father, who loved us and by his grace gave us
eternal encouragement and good hope,
encourage your hearts and strengthen you
in every good deed and word.*

2 Thessalonians 2:16-17 NIV

In 2003, my children were attending a private Christian school in another county, so we moved to an area closer to their school. Two years later, I started to go through menopause, and the hormonal changes put me into a deep depression. It got so bad that I couldn't even get out of bed. Unfortunately, I was not living a Christian life at that time; I had gotten far removed from having a relationship with the Lord. Then, my younger son and daughter decided they wanted to live with my ex-husband. So, in 2005, the two children moved in with their dad.

In the spring of 2006, I cried out to the Lord for help. I decided to start going to church again and to get counseling. I did not watch any TV that year; I only listened with great intent to Gospel music. A month later, I tried a new type of counseling called "trauma therapy," which was being offered by the church where my son attended school.

After my initial counseling interview, I was told that I had a lot of trauma as a little girl. I was assigned to three different counselors within the program, yet all three ended up saying they felt inadequate to handle my case. So, they put me in the care of the head counselor, who I'll call "Carol." At the same time, I wanted to attend a Sunday School class since I desperately wanted to develop spiritually. So, I asked a friend of mine at the church what class she thought would best suit my needs as a single, divorced mother. She told me about a class she thought would be a good fit.

As the class started, I walked into the room and sat down at a table. I was the only student there, but the teacher introduced herself to me. Finally, others started coming into the classroom as well, including one of my original three counselors. She looked over at me with a disdainful, condescending look, grabbed her Bible and notebook, and left the room, slamming the door behind her. She did not utter one word to me. I was uncomfortable and troubled that she made such a spectacle of me being there.

The next morning, I received a phone call from the head counselor asking me why I was in that Sunday School classroom. I told her that it had been recommended to me, so I went. She responded in very sharp tones that I was to never put my foot in that class again. I was dumbfounded but agreed. I took a moment and thought about what Jesus would have done in that same situation. He would have draped his shawl on the ground, picked me up, and carried me in the classroom to sit beside Him. Once again, I had been hurt and rejected.

A few days later, I wrote the counseling department a letter explaining that I did not mean to cause any harm or hurt anyone with my presence in a Sunday School class. It was not my intention to cause any trouble. I also added what I thought Jesus would have done and where was He in that situation. I never went back to Sunday School class there again.

19

Christian Counseling

If my people, who are called by my name, will humble themselves and pray and seek my face and turn from their wicked ways, then will I hear from heaven and will forgive their sin and will heal their land.

2 Chronicles 7:14 NIV

And the God of all grace, who called you to his eternal glory in Christ, after you have suffered a little while, will himself restore you and make you strong, firm and steadfast.

1 Peter 5:10 NIV

The head counselor at the church told me that I would never get well if I didn't attend a new kind of trauma release therapy, so I agreed to do so. The new type of counseling was very challenging for me. Carol had written a book on the method and how to use it to achieve the best results, and she told me to read it. When I did, I realized she was handling my therapy differently from what she had written in her book. I pointed out the specific passages that reflected a different approach than how she was conducting my sessions. I called her attention to them and showed her how she was taking my therapeutic measurements differently than she had specified in her book. She did not like that I drew her attention to how she handled my sessions.

I admit that I have always been strong-willed and very opinionated. I am the one in the crowd that makes sure things are done correctly. But from that point on, therapy with Carol was difficult and disruptive.

After a few months of meeting with Carol, she came into the room one day in a very argumentative mood. She virtually told me there was no hope for me, as she had ascertained that I could not be "healed," and I would no longer be her client. I realized she didn't really want to help me. She told me I had the worst personality disorder any client could have.

Then she went to the door and hollered out to the other staffers in the office that I had hit her.

I was stunned. I sat there in disbelief and told her that I did not hit her. I knew how to fight, and if I had hit her, she would have been on the floor covered in blood. Within a few minutes, the police arrived. One of the officers asked me if I had indeed hit her. I told him I had not, and he dismissed me to go home. A week later, two police officers came to my home and arrested me, informing me of two felony charges against me. I spent three days in jail sleeping on a thin mat on the floor outside of a cell room since the jail was severely overcrowded.

Nevertheless, even with the uncomfortable conditions I was dealing with—sleeping on the floor and eating bologna sandwiches—I had peace, knowing I had not done what I was accused of. I gladly talked with other people in the cells about my relationship with the Lord. I felt I was there for a reason, which was to give my fellow inmates hope in God, the very hope I experienced while being there.

Bail was posted, and I had to wait for a court-mandated hearing to see if the charges would be validated. Meanwhile, I was told I could no longer attend that church for any church services or go to any school functions held there. The private school my son was attending was at the same church. I was very disheartened, but at the same time, I knew I was innocent.

Now, this was the second time I had been barred from a church. From my perspective, a church is a body of participants who are seeking and receiving love and acceptance from one another. I did not receive that there.

The judge dismissed the charges against me based on the other party who brought forth the action against me. It was her decision to drop the case. God worked things out for me once again. So, I was able to attend my son's graduation, which took place on the church grounds. But the wounds I had received at that church remained with me for a long time. It took a few years for me to be able to forgive the people involved in that unfortunate calamity.

20

A New Beginning

But for you who revere my name,
the sun of righteousness will rise with healing in its wings.

Malachi 4:2 NIV

A few months later, I was given a referral to see Sarah, another therapist. I'll never forget my first interview with her. She asked me to write down all the hurts in my heart, and I needed two pieces of paper to list them all. It was like I was trying to tell her not to see me because I had too much wrong with me. When she asked when I wanted to make another appointment to work on my issues, I was truly surprised that she was willing to continue to see me. I can tell you I have never met a kinder, more genuine person.

After every session, Sarah would pray with me. I wanted to learn more about her God. She gave me hope and showed me nothing but understanding, compassion, and the love of God I so desired.

I spent about six years receiving her counsel, and it paid off. Now I have "her" God, the amazing God she would talk about, the God she told me loved me from the very beginning.

Sarah referred me to a psychiatrist who prescribed an antidepressant medication for my severe depression. I was also given the diagnosis of post-traumatic stress disorder (PTSD) and other forms of mental illnesses from my psychiatrist due to the childhood abuses I endured. PTSD is a sickness in which a person has difficulty recovering after suffering a terrifying or traumatic event or incident. My symptoms often included repeated flashbacks and nightmares of what happened to me at an early age. Plus, I experienced agitation, irritability, hostility, hypervigilance, and self-destructive behaviors as well as being socially isolated. But even after 2006, I tried several times to end my life and was hospitalized in a psychiatric ward.

I told Sarah I just could not "perform" Christianity. She replied with utter certainty that I didn't have to. She said, "Just relax and let Jesus do it within you."

Those words of wisdom opened the doors to my freedom. I no longer felt I had to work to get close to God. I am still learning to rely on Jesus to do the changing within me as I totally surrender to Him.

21

Jesus Tidying Up

Fear not, for I have summoned you by name; you are mine.

Isaiah 43:1 NIV

Seeking approval and acceptance had been my main occupation in life. After having been rejected and abandoned so many times, I wanted nothing more than to be wanted.

At the same time, my sense of self-worth was about as low as it could go. As a little girl, I declared I was not going to let anyone hurt me again. But I didn't have to get hurt from others. I was doing a great job of hurting myself with feelings of guilt, remorse, and shame. I lived a lifetime holding onto resentment and did not know how to forgive myself.

My relationship with the Lord back then was strained; still, He kept pursuing me. I was scared—fearful of life and fearful of God. I could give Him only a little bit of room in my life at a time.

I was like a house made of bricks with lots of rooms in it. When I knew God was visiting one room, wanting to clean it up, I would close the door to that room. I'd let God tidy up just a little at a time—one room at a time—and then I'd let Him visit another room. He would just have access to portions of the house at a time, never the full house. Not until years later. Now I see the hand of God working on my behalf, cleaning me up so I could become the person He planned for me to be. Looking back, I can see that, with great patience, He came in and healed many difficult areas of my life. With His gentleness, through each hurt and wound I had, He drew me closer and closer to Him. Through each juncture in my life, I have become more in a position to receive greater love from Him.

As a little girl, I heard that God loves us. But back then, I thought, if He loves me, why does He let bad things happen to me? That proved He didn't love me. After all, my parents didn't love me, so why should I expect God to? But I had it backward. God loved me in spite of my frailties and not being able to love Him back.

During this healing period, little by little, my emotions caught up with my mind about God's love for me. During my "yahoo" moments, I would feel loved by God and would be tickled pink. With gradual acceptance, I could even tell Him on occasion that I loved Him back. Being loved by God in the darkest and most secret parts of my mind and heart was such a good, comforting feeling.

Satan didn't like me loving God. Many, many times I had to go deeper spiritually and do spiritual warfare. I would seek God and would pray a lot for guidance and discernment. But Satan, like a little bird, so cute, sitting on my shoulder, reminded me of what a horrible person I was and what repulsive things I had done and thought. God could not possibly love me, he told me. Many times, I believed those lies straight from the pit of hell.

Rebecca used to talk with me about spiritual warfare, and I knew firsthand it was reality. I read enough about it in the Bible to ascertain one thing for sure—whatever you think about most will control your life. A person's thought life certainly determines their behavior.

Through all my struggles, I wanted God. But for many years, by no stretch of the imagination could I see how much He wanted me. Wow! The mere thought of God wanting me is something to this day that is hard for my mind wrap itself around. How grateful I am that He chose me and didn't wait for me to choose Him first. God's purposes or plans are never thwarted by anyone or anything. Although things looked bleak at many points in my life, despite myself, God had his forces at work in me.

22

My Story

This is what the Lord, the God of Israel, says: "Write in a book all of the words I have spoken to you."

Jeremiah 30:2 NIV

The reason I am writing my story is to show the love of Jesus Christ. Yes, much of my life was spent in dismay and adversity.

Bad things happened, and I made a lot of bad choices with no one to blame but myself. My sin nature flourished as I chose to walk with the desire to sin. I was selfish and wanted to control my own destiny. I wanted to design my own life and not allow anyone, especially family or any adult, to deviate me from becoming who I thought I should be.

In sin, I fell hard. I was totally out of the will of God. Even while I was living in a rebellious, sinful lifestyle God still pursued me faithfully. The concealing, hiding layers of all my fears, problems, and corrupt ways was in Jesus' death on the cross. He paid for my every sin, all my sins, on the rugged cross.

But it is the deep desire of my heart to offer you the hope that is only found in Jesus Christ. Like me, recovery is in the realm of being transformed through the written word of God and in being in a relationship with Jesus Christ. Reading the word made me aware of God's fulfillment of the truth, hope and the grace offered freely through salvation.

I was an angry person, but God took that anger and made good come out of it. As they say, He took my mess and made it my message. I ran away from God. I thought He would hurt me and cause extra pain. But he kept pursuing me with love, not punishment.

I often heard the conviction and hope of the Holy Spirit in my mind. As the song says, through it all, I've learned to trust in Jesus, I've learned to trust in God and to depend on His word. But God...brought me, through it all!

Today I live in the peace of God and have a joy that's beyond words. God came in and took all my shame and gave me beauty for ashes. I finally have love for myself, and even more love for Him.

23

God's Love

*For he chose us in him before the creation of the world to
be holy and blameless in his sight. In love he predestined
us to be adopted as his sons through Jesus Christ, in accordance
with his pleasure and will – to the praise of his glorious
grace, which he has freely given us in the One he loves.*

Ephesians 1:4-6 NIV

One of my favorite scriptures is Isaiah 55:8, which says that
God's ways are not our ways. His thoughts are not our thoughts.
I see now that God knew every moment of my life, and every
time I pushed Him away, He persistently showed and brought
His love to me. Many times, He knew I was unable to accept
this love, and He continually brought it openly and readily to
me until I could receive it. God's love came into my heart and
mind in little fragments, piece by piece.

He was quite aware of my inability to receive His love. Yes,
He knows my inner being, for He created me. He didn't reject

me because I rejected Him. He never condemned me, but He graciously stood beside me while I was in despair and in pain. Music has always softened my heart toward God when nothing else could. Through praise music, I can open my heart to God and allow the words to be my prayer to Him.

This very day, I can totally submit to God's will. I can put my total trust in Him. Most every day, in my spirit, I crawl up in His lap and I sit there as His everlasting arms hold me.

Instead of spending only seconds in His arms, I can sit there for hours. Amazing grace and His triumphant love for me endures forever.

He has taken me from the miry clay of fear, confusion, and hurt and set my feet upon the Rock, Jesus, the lover of my soul. I will never let go of that Rock, as He will never let go of me!

Going through Jesus is the only way to get to the Father. I now belong to all three—God the Father, Jesus my Savior and Lord, and the Holy Spirit to guide and comfort me.

It is His amazing grace that He took me and has allowed me to love Him back. What a blessing!

Another of my favorite scriptures is Jeremiah 29:11: "'...for I know the plans I have for you,' declares the Lord, 'plans to prosper you, not to harm you, plans to give you a hope and a future.'"

I now have hope and a future throughout all my pain! Even that which seems bad is for good! What an everlasting and unchangeable love God has for us! The scripture from Romans 8:37-39, says it with complete meaning of my life. "Yet in all these things we are more than conquerors through Him who loved us. For I am persuaded that neither death nor life, nor angels nor principalities nor powers, nor things present nor things to come, nor height nor depth, nor any other created thing, shall be able to separate us from the love of God which is in Christ Jesus our Lord."

Even when I didn't want Him, it was God's desire of His own heart to show and give me love. And He continued to draw me to Him until I could see it and receive it.

24

Grateful

For God so loved the world that he gave his on and only Son,
that whoever believes in him shall not perish but have eternal life.
For God did not send his Son into the
world to condemn the world,
but to save the world through him.

John 3:16-17 NIV

I am grateful for the many blessings His love has poured out on me.

I now have a church that identifies with hurts, wounds, and recovery and people there who are willing to help others through their pain.

I recently discovered some wonderful family members I didn't know I had and I got to meet them for the first time. One of them is Carla, a special cousin. We share the same biological grandfather, but we did not know we were related until five years ago.

Carla has truly been a blessing to me. She accepted me with all my hurts, frailties, and pain. She and I hang out on a regular basis with one another. Again, God put the right person in my life at the right time. Through Carla, I have received genuine love, compassion, and more knowledge of God. Imagine! A family member loving me! My walk with the Lord has greatly flourished because of her sincere counsel and guidance. She has pointed me to the cross of Jesus at various times in many situations. Carla has given me hope.

During my life, I was blessed to have four children, although I lost one in the womb. Through all my struggles, my son Christian gave me unconditional love and remained very close to me as he was growing up. Children can get caught up in the mix of their parents' fussing and arguing with one another. But, even as a little boy, Christian would depend on me and honor me. I had the privilege of coaching him in basketball and baseball while he was growing up.

We were very close and spent a lot of time together. He included me in his life. At that time, I didn't see unconditional love from anyone else but Christian. He always made me feel very special.

To this day, Christian still loves me unconditionally and involves me with his family. Though he was reared by a parent who was often confused and perplexed, today he is in the ministry as a lead pastor, spreading God's good news of grace, salvation, and love. I am so genuinely proud of him, his wife, and three children, all of whom love the Lord.

I am so grateful and honored that I am my grandchildren's Mimi. Again, the Word of God does not return void and prayers were answered that God enlightened Christian's pathway to the way, truth, and the life.

25

Calling from God

Praise be to the God and Father of our Lord Jesus Christ! In his great mercy he has given us new birth into a living hope through the resurrection of Jesus Christ from the dead, and into an inheritance that can never perish, spoil or fade-kept in heaven for you, who through faith are shielded by God's power until the coming of the salvation that is ready to be revealed in the last time. In this you greatly rejoice, though now for a little while you may have had to suffer grief in all kinds of trials. These have come so that your faith—of greater worth than gold, which perishes even though refined by fire—may be proved genuine and may result in praise, glory and honor when Jesus Christ is revealed. Though you have not seen him, you love him; and even though you do not see him now, you believe in him and are filled with an inexpressible and glorious joy, for you are receiving the goal of your faith, the salvation of your souls.

1 Peter 1:3-9 NIV

*T*o those without hope, I want to encourage you to put your hope in the Lord. God's love is faithful and will endure for eternity. Take heart. He is calling you out of your hurts, your wounds, and your anger, unto Himself. God doesn't need you, *but* He wants you.

He has given me a life filled with blessings, such as love, friendship, guidance, and His righteousness. I know He wants to fill your life with blessings and guidance as well.

He is a big God, ready to heal both large and small wounds, hurts, and painful memories. He wants to show you how to cope with anger and bitterness as He has done for me.

I can now say I am "growing up" in the Lord. Today I can say I have no anger or bitterness—none! As He reveals Himself to me, I have learned to receive more love from Him. God has taken away my self-pity for the loss of a childhood without parents who loved me. I no longer have a victim mentality, but one that is victorious in Jesus Christ. As difficult as it was growing up, I had to give it up to move forward. I let go of the ashes and my joy is forever.

In 2016, I was at the beach in Panama City visiting with my sister. Sitting in a chair on the beach, I heard God say to me, "Debbie, I love you. Do you see the sand on this beach?"

"Yes, Lord," I said.

He said, "My love for you is more than all the sand on this beach. It is more than the sand on all the beaches in the world. It is more than all the sand in all the oceans. I love you that much. Just receive it."

I was feeling so overwhelmed by our conversation I started crying. Because of my past, I hardly ever cried. His love so softened my heart, so overwhelmed me that tears flowed. I believed the good news. It completely saturated my heart, mind, and soul.

Little by little, all during my life, amid my anger, I have been receiving His gracious tokens of love.

In 2017, I spent a weekend in the Georgia Mountains at an event called Tres Dias. While there, God truly met me at my point of need. It was a continuation of my journey of restoration by His grace. The theme song was "Clean," sung by Natalie Grant on CD.

I see shattered, you see whole.
I see broken, but you see beautiful.
And you're helping me to believe,
You're restoring me, piece by piece.
There's nothing too dirty that you can't make worthy
You wash me in mercy, I am clean.
What was dead now lives again.
My heart's beating inside my chest
Oh, I'm coming alive with joy and destiny.
Cause you're restoring me, piece by piece.
Washed in the blood of your sacrifice.
Your blood flowed red and made me white.
My dirty rags are purified, I am clean.

The lyrics of that song penetrated my heart and mind. I am so thankful that God is restoring me piece by piece.

That whole weekend, I literally basked in His presence and love, and I had another experience with God's healing hands. I will always treasure that time with the Lord; it was a touch of heaven for me! I am thrilled that God chose me to attend, for it was His perfect timing!

In the past, I often couldn't handle the concept of God wanting to love me and I rejected it. But God kept pursuing me. On another day, I sat quietly before Him as He told me that I belong. I belong to God! I felt that I finally had a family and belonged to someone. I felt wonderful as I accepted being finally wanted.

His amazing grace and healing have made my pain have value. God, in His mercy, His loving mercy, has given me the ability to love Him back when all these years I thought I was incapable of doing it.

I still run. But now, instead of running away, I run into the arms of my Almighty Father. He still woos me to Himself.

I don't live in a perfect world, but I live with a perfect Father, my Abba Father. I have the peace that passes all understanding. I've learned to carry all my hurts and worries and all my joy, to the Lord. Mourning turns to songs of praise!

Currently, as I read the passage in Deuteronomy 1:29-31 NIV, God reveals to me that He has done what He said He would do. He told me not to be terrified, not to be afraid! Now I see that God, going before me, many times fights for me as He did in the past. The scripture reports that my Lord, my God, carries me as a father carries his son. In His love, grace, and mercy, God carried me until finally I could love and want Him in return. My security and trust are in Him!

What comfort I have in God. What hope! Even as a grown woman, in my heart and mind, I crawl up and sit in my Daddy's arms. He wants that, as I do! He listens to me, and I am training myself to listen to Him.

Through everything, He still loves me as I have grown to love Him!

This is what I want for you, too—to know that, in His great grace, God loves you so much He will not leave nor forsake you.

I found hope, grace, and love in God! For I know this one thing: He is crazy about me—and you!

Confession with repentance of one's sins is the bridge to allowing Jesus into your heart and having God bring wholeness, completeness, cleansing, and healing within your heart, mind, and soul.

Psalm 51 NIV, is an example of David's pouring out his heart for that healing of his brokenness. David was a man after God's heart. Let me remind you that he had just committed murder and adultery. But because of David repentance of those sins and willingness to humble himself, God mercifully and graciously forgave him.

Use this Psalm as a starting point when dealing with any sense of distance from your Father or dealing with guilt that is affecting your relationship with Him. Remember, no sin is too great to be forgiven! God can and will forgive you of all your sins. I know because He has for me!

Quietly say these words:
Have mercy on me, O God,
according to your unfailing love;
according to your great compassion
blot out my transgressions.
Wash away all my iniquity
and cleanse me from my sin.
For I know my transgressions,
and my sin is always before me.
Against you, you only, have I sinned
and done what is evil in your sight,
so that you are proved right when you speak
and justified when you judge.
Surely, I was sinful at birth,
sinful from the time my mother conceived me.
Surely you desire truth in the inner parts;
you teach me wisdom in the inmost place.
Cleanse me with hyssop, and I will be clean;
wash me, and I will be whiter than snow.
Let me hear joy and gladness;
let the bones you have crushed rejoice.
Hide your face from my sins
and blot out all my iniquity.
Create in me a pure heart, O God,
and renew a steadfast spirit within me.
Do not cast me from your presence
or take your Holy Spirit from me.
Restore to me the joy of your salvation
and grant me a willing spirit, to sustain me.

Then I will teach transgressors your ways,

and sinners will turn back to you.

Save me from bloodguilt, O God,

the God who saves me,

and my tongue will sing of your righteousness.

O Lord, open my lips,

and my mouth will declare your praise.

You do not delight in sacrifice, or I would bring it;

you do not take pleasure in burnt offerings.

The sacrifices of God are a broken spirit;

a broken and contrite heart.

O God, you will not despise.

In your good pleasure make Zion prosper;

build up the walls of Jerusalem.

Then there will be righteous sacrifices,

whole burnt offerings to delight you;

then bulls will be offered on your altar.

As you offer your prayer of repentance in the name of Jesus, God will come into your heart and thus your journey with Him will begin anew. For God is in the business of restoration and reconciliation unto Himself. To this day, I can cheerfully boast that I have been graciously healed by God. I no longer must take antidepressant medicines, and I no longer suffer from symptoms of PTSD. I know the Healer and am so very grateful of what He has done in my life.

Seek God first and foremost, then the rest of your life will fall into place, being restored piece by piece. For Jesus loves you. This I know, for the Bible told me so!

*"The Lord your God is with you; he is mighty to save.
He will take great delight in you, he will quiet you
with his love, he will rejoice over you with singing"*

Zephaniah 3:17 NIV

I finally and with great pleasure believe that He does love me! And it's awesome knowing He is for me! May God bless you as you walk the true, abundant life that is only found in Him!

For the grace of God has appeared, bringing salvation for all people, training us to renounce ungodliness and worldly passions, and to live self-controlled, upright, and godly lives in the present age, waiting for our blessed hope, the appearing of the glory of our great God and Savior Jesus Christ, who gave himself for us to redeem us from all lawlessness and to purify for himself a people for his own possession who are zealous for good works.

Titus 2:11-14 ESV.

26

One More Trial

I remember my affliction and my wandering, the bitterness and the gall. I well remember them, and my soul is downcast within me. Yet this I call to mind and therefore I have hope; Because of the LORD's great love we are not consumed, for his compassions never fail. They are new every morning; great is your faithfulness.

Lamentations 3:19-23 NIV

This year has been very, difficult, and nonetheless bewildering year for me. It was a time of tremendous uncertainty. Today, I hold onto the Scriptures and the promises given in the Bible about trials and tribulations that will happen. However, being perfectly honest with you, I failed. I failed miserably. I stumbled as I even allow this to happen, especially knowing how this specific sin has affected me all my life. God allows bad situations to arise to see what is being revealed in one's heart. Trust me, mine was not at all pretty. Typically, during my trials, I learned to see God in a newer, deeper way.

In October 2018, when I was at work, I was sexually assaulted by a man who had professed his Christianity to me. I failed to see God in the midst of this trial, and I put the emphasis on the actual sin itself. I got angry at God and questioned why it had to occur in the first place.

Pride reared its ugly head in me as I had the nerve to question God about it. And yes, I did question it. But God was indeed patient and longsuffering to allow me to have my pity party. Even though He did not dance with me during it, He loved me during it.

In our walk with God, we need to saturate the truths and expose ourselves to God's Word. We need to develop Bible-based convictions. Convictions are something you believe so strongly that it affects the way you live. Our convictions and values come from two places: from the world's standards or from the renewal of our minds by the Word of God.

> *Blessed is the man who walks not in the counsel of the wicked, nor stands in the way of sinner, nor sits in the seat of scoffers; but his delight is in the law of the LORD, and on his law he meditates day and night. He is like a tree planted by streams of water that yields its fruit on its season, and its leaf does not wither. On all that he does, he prospers.*
>
> *Psalm 1:1-3 ESV*

The Psalmist says that there are two groups of people: those who walk wickedly and those who delight in the law of God. However, believers are probably being captivated and influenced by both society standards and by the Word of God. The Psalmist gives us the truth in Verse 2: his delight is in the law of the Lord and on his law, he meditates day and night. That should be our attitude toward the Word of God. Ask yourself if you are willing to meditate on God's Word day and night. Whatever you do think or meditate dictates your way of life.

To meditate on the Word means to think about a truth with a view to its meaning and then to apply the truth to one's life. Sowing the Word deep within brings joy and peace, even through a storm, when one keeps their focus on God and His Word. Allow the scriptures to guide you into interpreting the difficult trials in your life. Trials and temptations will happen.

> *The book of the Law shall not depart from your mouth, but you shall meditate on it day and night, so that you may be careful to do according to all that is written in it. For then you will make your way prosperous, and then you will have good success. Have I not commanded you? Be strong and courageous. Do not be frightened, and do not be dismayed, for the Lord your God is with you wherever you go.*
>
> *Joshua 1:8-9 ESV*

Nonetheless I was thoroughly undone as I journeyed through one more trial of sexual assault. It was horrifying and repulsive to me and for a while, I lost connection to the truth that God was with me. I didn't meditate on the scriptures to bring me healing to change. Romans 12:2 ESV states, "Do not be conformed to this world, but be transformed by the renewal of your mind, that by testing you may discern what is the will of God, what is good and acceptable and perfect."

We know that we are all going to sin and fall into a variety of trials and tribulations. But as believers in Christ, we are dead to sin and alive in God, as it says in Romans 6. Paul, once the hater of Christians, transformed and accepted Jesus as his Savior clearly responds to the concern in Romans 6. He wrote a whole chapter about the subject matter knowing that we all will have problems with that very issue from time to time in our lives. He wrote that the law does not and cannot conquer sin, but the grace given to followers of Christ triumphs over sin and death.

What shall we say then? Are we to continue in sin that grace may abound? By no means! How can we who died to sin still live on it? Do you not know that all of us who have been baptized into Christ Jesus were baptized into his death? We were buried therefore with him by baptism into death, in order that, just as Christ was raised from the dead by the glory of the Father, we too might walk in newness of life. For if we have been united with him in a death like his, we shall certainly be united with him in a resurrection like his. We know that our old self was crucified with him in order that the body of sin might by brought to nothing so that we would no longer be enslaved to sin. For one who has died has been set free from sin. Now if we have died with Christ, we believe that we will also live with him. We know that Christ, being raised from the dead, will never die again.: death no longer has dominion over him. For the death he died he died to sin, once for all, but the life he lives he lives to God. So, you also must consider yourselves dead to sin and alive to God in Christ Jesus. Let not sin therefore reign in your mortal body, to make you obey its passions. Do not present your members to sin as instruments for unrighteousness but present yourselves to God as those who have been brought from death to life, and your members to God as instruments for righteousness. For sin will have no dominion over you, since you are not under law but under grace.

Romans 6:1-13 NIV

Paul went on to say that just because you are a Christian does not give you the right to keep sinning. He emphatically rejected the idea that freedom from the law implies that you can fulfill the sins of the flesh. Moral decisions still count for believers. It's important to give oneself wholly to God rather to sin.

Many times, like David, I also chose to become cynical during that unbearable time, and I am not excusing that fact. But God! God chose to listen to the cries of my heart. I will again use the Psalm as a hymn of personal thanksgiving for God's care during that specific circumstance.

I love the Lord, because he has heard my voice and my pleas for mercy. Because he inclined his ear to me, therefore I will call on him as long as I live. The snares of death encompassed me; the pangs of Sheol laid hold on me; I suffered distress and anguish. Then I called on the name of the Lord: "O Lord, I pray, deliver my soul!" Gracious is the Lord, and righteous; our God is merciful. The Lord preserves the simple; when I was brought low, he saved me. Return, O my soul, to your rest; for the Lord has dealt bountifully with you. For you have delivered my soul from death, my eyes from tears, my feet from stumbling; I will walk before the Lord in the land of the living. I believed even when I spoke; I am greatly afflicted"; I said in my alarm, "All mankind are liars." What shall I render to the Lord for all his benefits to me? I will lift the cup of salvation and call on the name of the Lord, I will pay my vows to the Lord in the presence of all his people. Precious in the sight of the Lord is the death of his saints. O Lord, I am your servant; I am your servant, the son of your maidservant. You have loosed my bonds. I will offer to you the sacrifice of thanksgiving and call on the name of the Lord. I will pay my vows to the Lord in the presence of all his people, in the courts of the house of the Lord in your midst, O Jerusalem. Praise the Lord!

Psalm 116:1-19 ESV

He heard the cry from my heart, not from my failure but from the need of a Savior. He gave me deliverance from impending death and in the time of dire need. As I was at my lowest point, and because of His genuine love and faithfulness, He saved me from my anguish and despair. After confession and repentance to being self-sufficient, I had to ask myself if I was willing to allow the truths and scriptures to guide me back to the truth of who God is and His purposes for my life. Philippians 1:6 ESV clearly states: "and I am sure of this, that He who began a good work in you will bring it to completion of the day of Jesus Christ."

That is the blessed assurance that when God starts something within you, He will complete it, no matter how much you fight against it at times with your pity parties and rebel heart. I am personally learning the application of His grace on a daily basis. I am grateful that we serve a God that won't give up, even when we do! I saw my sinful heart, and I needed growth and change. My lack of vision, self-sufficiency, and pride were no less of a sin than that person that inflicted his sinful desires on me.

Upon dealing with sin ask yourselves these questions:

Are the truths of Scriptures changing you?

Are you applying the truths that you learned in your walk with God?

Do you see life through the grid of the scriptures? Are you growing through the sanctification process?

Lastly, but equally important: Is your focus on God and not the trial itself?

During this last tragedy, I learned a vital and important lesson in my Christian walk. I learned to keep my absolute focus on God rather than on all the "why's" I could muster. I was so disappointed with myself that I allowed this traumatic experience to reign above my love and desire for God. I could not see His purpose as to why He allowed it to happen, yet I could not cloud my highest desire to give Him the glory during the storm.

But God! God took my failure and set me on His high! Once again, He was very patient with me. That is why I want to tell you, too, that when your trials come—and they will—look unto the Most High and search your heart for exactly what you need to learn and what needs to be changed within.

I am so grateful that I had my church family, Laurie, and my pastor Chris by my side to bring me hope and encouragement during that time. Chris suggested that I receive biblical counseling and I knew that I needed it. Of all my years being engaged in counseling, nothing remotely came close to the journey I was embarked upon with this type of counseling. This biblical counseling was truly ordained by God Himself.

I met with Debra, a biblical counselor. Her assiduous attention to the details in the ministry helped me in many facets of my life, including spiritually and emotionally. During our weekly sessions, Debra offered me knowledge of a deeper, more intimate revelation of my union only found in Jesus Christ through the power of the Gospel. She gained her wisdom from a personal experience of the Holy Spirit lifting the veil from her own eyes and heart. For me, a newfound heart and transformation from God were received along with restorative answers.

I deeply needed to hear Debra's profound, reflective, and practical approach to the many issues and struggles I was dealing with. She made it easier for me to delight in and have the aspiration of captivating the spiritual truths into my everyday life. She told me that I had a "heart" problem that needed to be taken care of as soon as possible. God arranged an outcome through Debra that I could no longer have the control that could not expose my sinful, evil heart.

The first Scripture she counseled me with was found in Jeremiah 17: 9. It captured the dynamics of a "biblical" change for me. That scripture specifically addresses the fact that the heart is very deceitful. Now, the word "deceitful" means guilty of or involving deceit; deceiving, deception, or misleading others. Other meanings are: being untruthful, lying, dishonesty, and trickery. Within the heart lies a distortion of the truth, according to the Bible. The toxicity of my heart was so potent that I was deceived into thinking that I was living a wonderful Christian life and that I had a good relationship with the Lord. With a deep magnitude and keen sensitivity of the significance of a continuing, growing knowledge and intimacy with God, Debra fervently and zealously counseled me.

I knew Debra was right on target. I was convicted by the Holy Spirit as to what needed to be addressed. The Holy Spirit is the glue and foundational weapon for what God uses to express His power in action. Read Micah 3:8 and Luke 1:35, as God pro-fesses his power through the Holy Spirit. God sends out His Spirit by projecting his energy to any place or person to accomplish His will. I privately asked Him why it took so long to let me know about going through this much needed biblical and spiritual healing. The answer I quickly received was that I had not been ready to hear the news about needing change, nor had I been ready to let go of controlling my life. In other words, I was not at all able to willingly submit or humble myself before God for any change. Change of the heart requires humility and the willingness to surrender control of one's life.

Jeremiah 17:5-8 gives a perfect analogy for needing change by comparing two trees:

This is what the Lord says:

Cursed is the person who trusts in mankind.
He makes human flesh his strength,
and his heart turns from the Lord.
He will be like a juniper in the Arabah;
He cannot see when good comes
But dwells in the parched places in the wilderness,
In a salt land where no one lives.
The person who trusts in the LORD,
Whose confidence indeed is the LORD, is blessed.
He will be like a tree planted by water:
It sends its roots out toward a stream,
It doesn't fear when heat comes,
And its foliage remains green.
It will not worry in a year of drought
Or cease producing fruit.

Jeremiah 17:5-8 ESV

The first tree represents a person who puts their trust in other humans, and who is isolated, dry, and barren like a juniper tree. The second tree is continually flowing since it is drawing water from a reliable source, as does someone who puts his trusts in the Lord. Conclusively, when we humbly submit to spiritual growth, and with the Holy Spirit's guidance, change will occur. A new path toward becoming Christlike is inevitable.

But I was way too busy worshipping the idols of my evil heart to allow God to be sovereign. God awakened my heart within the depths of His grace and love for me. His love changed my rebel heart to fuel my desire for that change. My heart was permeated with loathsome sins and filled with evil passions. During my biblical counseling sessions with Debra, she helped me understand why I believed the way I did. I did not know the real, genuine spiritual truths about God. I knew from the teaching of my adopted parents that God was a god of "do's" and "don'ts." I did not have a true, honest, or relevant relationship with Him. My views about God had been distorted as a young girl, so I will always remember fearing God in an unhealthy way and holding Him at bay all my life. Fear brought in self-interest and pride. Instead of a devout, faithful relationship filled with love, the heaviness of wickedness easily resided within me. I was determined to keep God at a distance for my own protection. I was being my own god: I was rebellious, prideful, controlling, and unbelieving. I did not have peace but remained embattled with Him, privately fighting within myself and overcome by all sorts of feelings and emotions about God.

27

Convictions of the Heart

I confess my iniquity; I am troubled by my sin. Psalm 38:18 NIV.
It was good for me to be afflicted so that
i might learn your decrees.

Psalm 119:71 NIV

Debra provided me with spiritual truths from the Word that slowly began to resonate in my mind and then in my heart, too. She also gave me a list of books to read to assist my process. Each book was written to show the character of Jesus and to guide us to be more like Him. One book described my identity in Christ as I embraced and sorely desired wanting to be valued by God. Every book seemed to be designed by the Holy Spirit, helping me transform my heart.

In my previous spiritual walks, many times I wanted to be in right standing with the Lord, but I did not know how to make the changes to do so. I yearned with hopeful, grateful anticipation that change would occur somehow. I had been living my life through self-effort, self-dependency, self absorbtion, self righteousness, and self-control. My spiritual foundation had been built on false doctrines rather than on the truths of Jesus Christ. The more sessions I attended, the more scriptures, precepts, and truths I listened to with a burning desire to know who God really was.

I soon became very aware that for me to find out who God was would take growth in the knowledge of the Trinity. I also became aware of the fact that I could not produce the power and willingness to bring about a spiritual change all by myself. With the help of the biblical counseling, my reading, and the many prayers being prayed, the desires within my heart started to change. The Holy Spirit demanded and forced me to become honest and realistic. I was forced to recognize that I could no longer put the blame on my past; I was finally being completely accountable for how my life had erupted into one mess after another.

Then the Holy Spirit showed me that I had to repent my life-long anger toward God. I had to recognize that I was prideful, rebellious, and had been maintaining a high level of irreverence toward Him. I could no longer push it under the rug and hide from it. I had done so much that I thought I was just fine with God running along with my happy, but miserable self. I was deceived by the severity and true complexity of all the wickedness within me.

But God showed me small glimpses of my real heart—nasty and vile as it was! I was crushed and distraught and troubled about it. I wondered how God could love me with such a heart. How could I even hope for a pinch of His love? How in the world could I change? But I was reminded that, indeed, that was the reason Jesus was born in human flesh, died, and arose from death—to give each of us eternal life with Him.

The more I saw the ugly truth about my heart, the more meaning His death and resurrection meant to me. Finally! The more I read about how He lived a perfect life, gave His life up for me on the cross, the more I wanted change. Again, I knew that I would not be able to transform my own heart. Several times a day I cried out to God to bring about that change. At the same time, I wanted to check my motives for wanting that change. I wanted to make sure I had only a pure, genuine desire for His glory. Yet at the same time, an incredible amount of anger toward God would raise its ugly head inside of me from time to time. I was dealing with different entities spiritually and fighting the battle of wanting to be in control of my life.

Oh, happy day! Since November 3, 2018, I've had great and deeply-felt convictions of the heart.

On July 27, 2019, as I was working, and while my client was fast asleep, God quickened my spirit and told me it was time to give up all my false idols. I cried, asking Him for forgiveness as I gave Him the reins to take complete control of my life. Can the urge to want control back, to be prideful and angry, or to have other idols of the heart be reckoned with at one time? Absolutely not. It's a decision you make each day to thwart giving to God. But the power of the Holy Spirit will combat those evil desires if you walk in the Spirit and not the flesh. Each morning, I start by asking God for His help. With determination, I put my trust in Him and not myself. I say, "Lord, I give my total being in words and in actions to your control and your will, not mine. God, please, guide my every step."

God was patient with me and proved His love for me. He allowed me to continue to live in my sins. The Bible gives specific teaching on how to address someone who is wrong doctrinal or in sin, as in Galatians 5:25-26 and Galatians 6:1. I have been restored in the spirit of meekness both with God and in my biblical counseling. The manner of confrontation stemmed from love that gave me the desire to want change even more. Both my surface sins and the heart issue had to be dealt with to usher in change.

In the Old Testament, the Israelites were refused entrance to the Promised Land because of "unbelief." I, as well, had to come to terms with my lack of belief. In Matthew 14:31, Jesus rebuked Peter of his state of unbelief. And I know it rests at the core of my anger, depression, immorality, and other vices that I engaged in due to the simple fact that I took my eyes off God as my real, true source of joy and provision. I was told that my sins were a manifestation of not being able to put my trust in God and not having the faith to believe. Again, I had to take owner-ship of not believing, confess it, and repent to God.

It was my prayer and desire that He would help me to believe in him. The lack of assurance of unbelief fueled the fire to not want God. Only when you can "rest" or abide within a complete assurance will you receive the fruits of a changed heart. Accepting the full responsibility of all these idols took time as I would draw back into the blame game because of my horrendous childhood and adulthood abuse. I called these offenses "idols" since I spent more time dwelling and thinking about them than I did worshipping God.

Within my counseling sessions, I was taught to look at life's problems and answers through the lens and grid of the scriptures. I was given a lot of information and interpretation from the scriptures that gave me the hope that change within my heart would occur. I know for a fact that God instilled within me the ability to embrace the truth of His Word. The book of Romans, chapters 6, 7, and 8 were heavily referenced and cited for my sanctification growth.

God's word in Isaiah 55:11 states that "my word...shall not return unto me void, but it shall accomplish that which I please, and it shall prosper in the thing where to send it." God clearly promises to bless His word to accomplish all the purposes He designed it for. Through the Holy Spirit, the Word, and my counselor, Debra, He gave me many foundational spiritual and biblical truths, that, with time, I became able to bear witness to. With a lot of meditation, and the wisdom from the Lord, the Word became my light through the deep darkness of my heart. God had to work in my heart for me to be able believe that He truly loved me. The hundreds of questions I asked in counseling were all consistently met with the wisdom of God's word, which ultimately brought about growth and change. My spiritual foundation that was once considered so weak began to be stronger and my heart began to change.

I had the hope, guidance, and desire to become what God had planned for my life all along. If anyone knows me privately, they know this fact: that I can ask a million questions on one topic alone. Once again, I asked God why it took all these years to learn these vital spiritual truths. And once again, the reply was, "Deborah, you were not ready. You could not hear the truth yet. My work had to be according to my timing, not yours."

Finally, my strong will was broken into a godly sorrow and I no longer wanted to control my life and be god of my life. It took the amazing power of the Holy Spirit for me to not desire to be in control any longer. I am actively being changed and want so desperately to be totally dependent upon God. I was clearly shown from the word that at this time my need for a Savior and Rescuer was desperately needed. As Paul describes in the book of Romans, I, as well, want to die in the flesh and allow the spirit man to dwell and abide in my Lord and Savior.

Ezekiel 36:26-27 ESV states this profound spiritual truth:

And I will give you a new heart, and a new spirit I will put within you. And I will remove the heart of stone from your flesh and give you a heart of flesh. And I will put my Spirit within you and cause you to walk in my statues and be careful to obey my rules.

During my journey with the Lord I am so grateful that he placed the right people in front of me at the right time, bringing me face to face with Him. Becoming transformed with a new heart has given me a great inner peace that I have never experienced before. With open arms, I gladly welcome a "love walk" with the utmost desire to please Him. Pleasing Him brings me such joy and comfort as I am only completely and wholly found in Him. God of endless mercies and unrelenting love brought me out of the dark prison of anger and rebellion toward Him into a freedom and liberty of knowing that I am loved by Him. He is ever so faithful keeping His promises of restoring his children.

As in Psalm 40:1-17 ESV, a plea from David reflects what occurred to me, too, as I cried out to God:

> *I waited patiently for the Lord, he inclined to me and heard my cry. He drew me up from the pit of destruction, out of the miry bog, and set my feet upon a rock, making my steps secure. He put a new song in my mouth, a song of praise to our God. Many will see and fear and put their trust in the Lord. Blessed is the man who makes the Lord his trust, who does not turn to the proud, to those who go astray after a lie! You have multiplied, O Lord my God, your wondrous deeds and your thoughts toward us; none can compare with you! I will proclaim and tell of them, yet they are more than can be told. In sacrifice and offering you have not delighted, but you have given me an open ear. Burnt offering and sin offering you have not required. Then I said, "Behold, I have come; in the scroll of the book it is written of me: I delight to do your will, O my God; your law is within my heart." I have told the glad news of deliverance in the great congregation; behold, I have not restrained my lips, as you know Lord. I have not hidden your deliverance within my heart; I have spoken of your faithfulness and your*

salvation; I have not concealed your steadfast love and your faithfulness from the great congregation. As for you, O Lord, you will not restrain your mercy from me; your steadfast love and your faithfulness will ever preserve me! For evils have encompassed me beyond number; my iniquities have overtaken me, and I cannot see; they are more than the hairs of my head; my heart fails me. Be pleased, O Lord, to deliver me! O Lord make haste to help me! Let those be put to shame and disappointed altogether who seek to snatch away my life; let those be turned back and brought to dishonor who delight in my hurt! Let those be appalled because of their shame who say to me, "Aha, Aha!" But may all who seek you rejoice and be glad in you; may those who love your salvation say continually, "Great is the Lord!" As for me, I am poor and needy, but the Lord takes thought for me. You are my help and my deliverer; do not delay, O my God!

Allow with the depth of your heart to cry out to him this Psalm and patiently watch for his deliverance! He will certainly establish your steps in his direction showing his grace in turning and hearing.

Be strong and keep your focus and vision on God! And love Him with all your heart, mind, and soul! You will become victorious in a lost and dying world! Just know that sanctification is a process—a daily one—but our God is more than enough to handle your every circumstance!

Remember this—as I have been told numerous times in counseling—Let God be God! The amazing and perfect God He is! God consistently wooed me with His reckless love and grace and no longer am I a rebel, but I am His beloved, chosen, and holy daughter! He rescued me from the pit of hell into His loving embrace piece by piece. For I am justified, redeemed, and found in Him!

In closing, Psalm 16:4,8,9, and verse 11 ESV talks about how:

> *the sorrows of those who run after another god shall multiply, (but) I have set the LORD always before me; because he is at my hand, I shall not be shaken. Therefore, my heart is glad, and my whole being rejoices; my flesh also dwells secure. You make known to me the path of life; at your right hand are pleasures forevermore.*

I know personally that it can be hard to accept His love; it was very difficult for me. I have asked him for many years for that revelation to make the flame bright in my heart, spiritually, emotionally, and mentally. I could not fathom the good news of the gospel of being loved by him. I even thought I tried to make it difficult for God to love me. However, He continued to reveal His love within His format and in His timing. His faithful, consistent, and endless love transformed my life bringing me a new keen awareness of my identity as a beloved child of God.

Grasping God's love provided me with hope as it challenged me to finally embrace the reality of a true, pure, and authentic sense of belonging and being wanted by Him. The gospel of good news made such a tangible impact on my heart and life. I mistakenly thought I had to fight to win his love and affection. The depth of His love for us stated in 1 John 4: 9-10 ESV:

> *In this the love of God was made manifest among us, that God sent his only Son into the world, so that we might live through him. In this is love, not that we have loved God but that he loved us and sent his Son to be the propitiation for our sins.*

The truth of the matter is that before the creation of the world, God created us in and through His love. His boundless love compelled me to have the desire to love Him back. With time and a lot of reading of the Word, I finally started to comprehend His endless and faithful love. Ultimately, God is not a respecter of persons, His love is ever so immeasurable and infinite.

HE NEVER GIVES UP!

He never gives up when you are at your wits end,
He never gives up when all your cares are about to bend.
He never gives up giving his heart full of love,
For that is sent from heaven above.
He never gives up whenever you see the rock bottom
come to despair,
So tenderly and oh so gently his mercy I declare.
When you reach out for an anchor to hold,
There is God there many times I have been told.
He never gives up as he often pursues,
For neither rhyme nor reason to conclude
That Almighty God will never give up!

28

Joy and Peace

I delight greatly in the LORD; my soul rejoices in my God.
For he has clothed me with garments of salvation and arrayed
me in a robe of righteousness, as a bridegroom adorns his head
like a priest, and as a bride adorns herself with her jewels.

Isaiah 61:10 NIV

My blessed friend, I know that God will never give up on you as He is patiently waiting for you this moment to fit the puzzle pieces of your life with love, forgiveness, and grace. If He continuously showed up for me, He will do the same for you, and I am forever grateful! Romans, Chapter 5:1-5 ESV, gives the assurance of unshakeable hope of being a Christ follower. I no longer live under the fear of judgement and the wrath of God but have continuous peace with Him. I have a hope of future glory and eternal life with God. Through my faith in Christ, I have been justified and declared righteous by God, once and for all. As you read these verses, please understand it's not just a feeling but an objective reality.

Therefore, since we, have been justified by faith, we have peace with God through our Lord Jesus Christ. Through him we have also obtained access by faith into this grace in which we stand, and we rejoice in hope of the glory of God. Not only that but we rejoice in our sufferings, knowing that suffering produces endurance, and endurance pro-duces character, and character produces hope, and hope does not put us to shame, because God's love has been poured into our hearts through the Holy Spirit who has been given to us. Romans 5:1-5 ESV

Finally, having Jesus come into my heart I knew that He fused Himself into the deepest parts of who I am. Christ literally unites His Spirit with ours. That means that Christ is in my heart as I submit to His Lordship. I now can praise God for the abuse that I have endured and am even thankful for the sexual assault of last October. Throughout my lifelong struggles and hardships, I can, with complete confidence and assurance, share in His glory!

I can fully trust God's complete sovereign power is and was being exercised on my behalf. All of my adversities were being controlled by God and used by Him in ways that His wisdom and love were dictated to me. As in Isaiah 40:10-11, I could

See, the Sovereign LORD comes with power, and his arm rules for him, See, His reward is with Him, and his recompense accompanies Him. He tends his flock like a shepherd: He gathers the lambs in his

arms and carries them close to his heart; he gently leads those that have young.

This is my comfort, my joy, and my peace that my all powerful, sovereign God shepherds me, watches me, and draws me into his faithful and tender arms. God's love will not ever fail as long as you put your trust in Him. As He firmly and continuously states in the Word, and says in Isaiah 54:10, "Though the mountains be shaken and the hills be removed, yet my unfailing love for you will not be shaken nor my covenant of peace be removed." So great is His unfailing love and compassion He has for you, and I believe that!

Lastly, I pray that you will have the desire to be captivated with the heartfelt delights of a rich and glorious inheritance of Jesus Christ, too! Determine to be compelled toward fully seeing the vision of God's inner beauty with the fulfillment of His presence within. Only this beauty can bring the joy and peace that you keenly desire. He changes, encourages, and motivates us with the security and reality of His love. Allow God to lead you into the dance of joyfulness by bringing you the transformation of the heart with Him piece by piece. Dance long and hard and be totally committed by seeking His faithful love and amazing, scandulous grace! Enter His rest and enjoy your journey! And let God be God of your life, filled with His burning and desiring love for YOU!!!!!

God bless YOU!!!

Deborah's Scriptures on "Who Am I in Christ?"

2 Corinthians 5:17 ESV

Therefore, if anyone is in Christ, he is a new creation. The old has passed away; behold, the new has come.

Ephesians 2:10 ESV

For we are his workmanship, created in Christ Jesus for good works, which God prepared beforehand, that we should walk in them.

1 Peter 2:9 ESV

But you are a chosen race, a royal priesthood, a holy nation, a people for his own possession, that you may proclaim the excellencies of him who called you out of darkness into his marvelous light.

Romans 8:1 ESV

There is therefore now no condemnation for those who are in Christ Jesus.

John 1:12 ESV

But to all who did receive him, who believed in his name, he gave the right to become children of God,

2 Corinthians 5:21 ESV

For our sake he made him to be sin who knew no sin, so that in him we might become the righteousness of God.

John 15:5 ESV

I am the vine; you are the branches. Whoever abides in me and I in him, he it is that bears much fruit, for apart from me you can do nothing.

1 Corinthians 6:19 ESV

Or do you not know that your body is a temple of the Holy Spirit within you, whom you have from God? You are not your own,

2 Timothy 1:7 ESV

For God gave us a spirit not of fear but of power and love and self-control.

John 15:15 ESV

No longer do I call you servants, for the servant does not know what his master is doing; but I have called you friends, for all that I have heard from my Father I have made known to you.

Galatians 3:26 ESV

For in Christ Jesus you are all sons of God, through faith.

Galatians 2:20 ESV

I have been crucified with Christ. It is no longer I who live, but Christ who lives in me. And the life I now live in the flesh I live by faith in the Son of God, who loved me and gave himself for me.

1 John 4:4 ESV

Little children, you are from God and have overcome them, for he who is in you is greater than he who is in the world.

Romans 12:2 ESV

Do not be conformed to this world, but be transformed by the renewal of your mind, that by testing you may discern what is the will of God, what is good and acceptable and perfect.

Philippians 4:13 ESV

I can do all things through him who strengthens me.

Philippians 3:20 ESV

But our citizenship is in heaven, and from it we await a Savior, the Lord Jesus Christ,

Romans 8:17 ESV

And if children, then heirs—heirs of God and fellow heirs with Christ, provided we suffer with him in order that we may also be glorified with him.

1 Corinthians 6:17 ESV

But he who is joined to the Lord becomes one spirit with him.

1 John 5:18 ESV

We know that everyone who has been born of God does not keep on sinning, but he who was born of God protects him, and the evil one does not touch him.

Romans 5:1 ESV

Therefore, since we have been justified by faith, we have peace with God through our Lord Jesus Christ.

1 Corinthians 12:27 ESV

Now you are the body of Christ and individually members of it.

Colossians 3:12 ESV

Put on then, as God's chosen ones, holy and beloved, compassionate hearts, kindness, humility, meekness, and patience.

1 Corinthians 3:16 ESV

Do you not know that you are God's temple and that God's Spirit dwells in you?

Ephesians 1:3 ESV

Blessed be the God and Father of our Lord Jesus Christ, who has blessed us in Christ with every spiritual blessing in the heavenly places.

Philippians 4:19 ESV

And my God will supply every need of yours according to his riches in glory in Christ Jesus.

John 15:16 ESV

You did not choose me, but I chose you and appointed you that you should go and bear fruit and that your fruit should abide, so that whatever you ask the Father in my name, he may give it to you.

2 Peter 1:4 ESV

By which he has granted to us his precious and very great promises, so that through them you may become partakers of the divine nature, having escaped from the corruption that is in the world because of sinful desire.

1 Peter 2:9-10 ESV

But you are a chosen race, a royal priesthood, a holy nation, a people for his own possession, that you may proclaim the excellencies of him who called you out of darkness into his marvelous light. Once you were not a people, but now you are God's people; once you had not received mercy, but now you have received mercy.

John 3:16 ESV

"For God so loved the world, that he gave his only Son, that whoever believes in him should not perish but have eternal life.

Ephesians 1:5 ESV

He predestined us for adoption as sons through Jesus Christ, according to the purpose of his will.

Psalm 139:14 ESV

I praise you, for I am fearfully and wonderfully made. Wonderful are your works; my soul knows it very well.

Colossians 3:3 ESV

For you have died, and your life is hidden with Christ in God.

Philippians 1:6 ESV

And I am sure of this, that he who began a good work in you will bring it to completion at the day of Jesus Christ.

Colossians 2:10 ESV

And you have been filled in him, who is the head of all rule and authority.

1 Corinthians 6:20 ESV

For you were bought with a price.

Matthew 5:14 ESV

You are the light of the world. A city set on a hill cannot be hidden.

Ephesians 1:7 ESV

In him we have redemption through his blood, the forgiveness of our trespasses, according to the riches of his grace.

Ephesians 3:12 ESV

In whom we have boldness and access with confidence through our faith in him.

1 Thessalonians 5:5 ESV

For you are all children of light, children of the day. We are not of the night or of the darkness.

Colossians 1:13 ESV

He has delivered us from the domain of darkness and transferred us to the kingdom of his beloved Son.

1 Corinthians 1:2 ESV

To the church of God that is in Corinth, to those sanctified in Christ Jesus, called to be saints together with all those who in every place call upon the name of our Lord Jesus Christ, both their Lord and ours.

2 Corinthians 5:20 ESV

Therefore, we are ambassadors for Christ, God making his appeal through us. We implore you on behalf of Christ, be reconciled to God.

John 14:6 ESV

Jesus said to him, "I am the way, and the truth, and the life. No one comes to the Father except through me.

John 15:1 ESV

"I am the true vine, and my Father is the vinedresser.

1 Corinthians 2:16 ESV

"For who has understood the mind of the Lord so as to instruct him?" But we have the mind of Christ.

Romans 8:37 ESV

No, in all these things we are more than conquerors through him who loved us.

Hebrews 4:16 ESV

Let us then with confidence draw near to the throne of grace, that we may receive mercy and find grace to help in time of need.

Matthew 5:13 ESV

You are the salt of the earth, but if salt has lost its taste, how shall its saltiness be restored? It is no longer good for anything except to be thrown out and trampled under people's feet.

Romans 8:28 ESV

And we know that for those who love God all things work together for good, for those who are called according to his purpose.

Ephesians 2:8-9 ESV

For by grace you have been saved through faith. And this is not your own doing; it is the gift of God, not a result of works, so that no one may boast.

Ephesians 1:4 ESV

Even as he chose us in him before the foundation of the world, that we should be holy and blameless before him.

Romans 6:23 ESV

For the wages of sin is death, but the free gift of God is eternal life in Christ Jesus our Lord.

Ephesians 1:1 ESV

Paul, an apostle of Christ Jesus by the will of God, To the saints who are in Ephesus, and are faithful in Christ Jesus.

Ephesians 2:18 ESV

For through him we both have access in one Spirit to the Father.

Colossians 2:7 ESV

Rooted and built up in him and established in the faith, just as you were taught, abounding in thanksgiving.

1 Peter 2:11 ESV

Beloved, I urge you as sojourners and exiles to abstain from the passions of the flesh, which wage war against your soul.

1 Peter 1:23 ESV

Since you have been born again, not of perishable seed but of imperishable, through the living and abiding word of God.

James 4:7 ESV

Submit yourselves therefore to God. Resist the devil, and he will flee from you.

1 Corinthians 1:30 ESV

And because of him you are in Christ Jesus, who became to us wisdom from God, righteousness and sanctification and redemption.

Colossians 1:14 ESV

In whom we have redemption, the forgiveness of sins.

1 Peter 2:5 ESV

You yourselves like living stones are being built up as a spiritual house, to be a holy priesthood, to offer spiritual sacrifices acceptable to God through Jesus Christ.

1 John 1:9 ESV

If we confess our sins, he is faithful and just to forgive us our sins and to cleanse us from all unrighteousness.

Galatians 4:6 ESV

And because you are sons, God has sent the Spirit of his Son into our hearts, crying, "Abba! Father!"

James 1:22 ESV

But be doers of the word, and not hearers only, deceiving yourselves.

Romans 10:9 ESV

Because, if you confess with your mouth that Jesus is Lord and believe in your heart that God raised him from the dead, you will be saved.

Acts 1:8 ESV

But you will receive power when the Holy Spirit has come upon you, and you will be my witnesses in Jerusalem and in all Judea and Samaria, and to the end of the earth.

Romans 6:18 ESV

And, having been set free from sin, have become slaves of righteousness.

Romans 6:6 ESV

We know that our old self was crucified with him in order that the body of sin might be brought to nothing, so that we would no longer be enslaved to sin.

Romans 3:24 ESV

And are justified by his grace as a gift, through the redemption that is in Christ Jesus.

2 Corinthians 2:14 ESV

But thanks be to God, who in Christ always leads us in triumphal procession, and through us spreads the fragrance of the knowledge of him everywhere.

Romans 8:2 ESV

For the law of the Spirit of life has set you free in Christ Jesus from the law of sin and death.

Romans 8:1-39 ESV

There is therefore now no condemnation for those who are in Christ Jesus. For the law of the Spirit of life has set you free in Christ Jesus from the law of sin and death. For God has done what the law, weakened by the flesh, could not do. By sending his own Son in the likeness of sinful flesh and for sin, he condemned sin in the flesh, in order that the righteous requirement of the law might be fulfilled in us, who walk not according to the flesh but according to the Spirit. For those who live according to the flesh set their minds on the things of the flesh, but those who live according to the Spirit set their minds on the things of the Spirit...

Ephesians 2:1 ESV

And you were dead in the trespasses and sins.

Ephesians 1:7-8 ESV

In him we have redemption through his blood, the forgiveness of our trespasses, according to the riches of his grace, which he lavished upon us, in all wisdom and insight.

Ephesians 2:5 ESV

Even when we were dead in our trespasses, made us alive together with Christ—by grace you have been saved.

Galatians 3:13 ESV

Christ redeemed us from the curse of the law by becoming a curse for us—for it is written, "Cursed is everyone who is hanged on a tree."

Romans 5:17 ESV

For if, because of one man's trespass, death reigned through that one man, much more will those who receive the abundance of grace and the free gift of righteousness reign in life through the one-man Jesus Christ.

1 Thessalonians 1:4 ESV

For we know, brothers loved by God, that he has chosen you.

Ephesians 4:24 ESV

And to put on the new self, created after the likeness of God in true righteousness and holiness.

Ephesians 2:13 ESV

But now in Christ Jesus you who once were far off have been brought near by the blood of Christ.

1 Corinthians 3:9 ESV

For we are God's fellow workers. You are God's field, God's building.

Romans 5:8 ESV

But God shows his love for us in that while we were still sinners, Christ died for us.

Colossians 1:22 ESV

He has now reconciled in his body of flesh by his death, in order to present you holy and blameless and above reproach before him.

Ephesians 5:8 ESV

For at one time you were darkness, but now you are light in the Lord. Walk as children of light.

1 Corinthians 6:19-20 ESV

Or do you not know that your body is a temple of the Holy Spirit within you, whom you have from God? You are not your own, for you were bought with a price. So glorify God in your body.

2 Corinthians 1:21 ESV

And it is God who establishes us with you in Christ and has anointed us.

2 Corinthians 1:22 ESV

And who has also put his seal on us and given us his Spirit in our hearts as a guarantee.

Philippians 4:6-7 ESV

Do not be anxious about anything, but in everything by prayer and supplication with thanksgiving let your requests be made known to God. And the peace of God, which surpasses all understanding, will guard your hearts and your minds in Christ Jesus.

Ephesians 1:6 ESV

To the praise of his glorious grace, with which he has blessed us in the Beloved.

2 Timothy 1:9 ESV

Who saved us and called us to a holy calling, not because of our works but because of his own purpose and grace, which he gave us in Christ Jesus before the ages began.

John 8:12 ESV

Again Jesus spoke to them, saying, "I am the light of the world. Whoever follows me will not walk in darkness, but will have the light of life."

Colossians 2:9-10 ESV

For in him the whole fullness of deity dwells bodily, and you have been filled in him, who is the head of all rule and authority.

2 Corinthians 2:15 ESV

For we are the aroma of Christ to God among those who are being saved and among those who are perishing.

Romans 12:3 ESV

For by the grace given to me I say to everyone among you not to think of himself more highly than he ought to think, but to think with sober judgment, each according to the measure of faith that God has assigned.

Romans 3:23 ESV

For all have sinned and fall short of the glory of God.

John 10:10 ESV

The thief comes only to steal and kill and destroy. I came that they may have life and have it abundantly.

1 John 5:14-15 ESV

And this is the confidence that we have toward him, that if we ask anything according to his will he hears us. And if we know that he hears us in whatever we ask, we know that we have the requests that we have asked of him.

Colossians 1:2 ESV

To the saints and faithful brothers in Christ at Colossae: Grace to you and peace from God our Father.

Galatians 5:1 ESV

For freedom Christ has set us free; stand firm therefore, and do not submit again to a yoke of slavery.

Deborah's Scriptures on "Who Does God Say I Am?"

I AM–A Child of God (Romans 8:16)

I AM–Redeemed from the Hand of the Enemy (Psalm 107:2)

I AM–Forgiven (Colossians 1:13, 14)

I AM–Saved by Grace through Faith (Ephesians 2:8)

I AM–Justified (Romans 5:1)

I AM–Sanctified (I Corinthians 6:11)

I AM–A New Creature (II Corinthians 5:17)

I AM–Partaker of His Divine Nature (II Peter 1:4)

I AM–Redeemed from the Curse of the Law (Galatians 3:13)

IAM–Delivered from the Powers of Darkness (Colossians 1:13) *I AM*–Led by the Spirit of God (Romans 8:14)

I AM–Free From All Bondage (John 8:36)

I AM–Kept in Safety Wherever I Go (Psalm 91:11)

I AM–Getting All My Needs Met by Jesus (Philippians 4:19)

I AM–Casting All My Cares on Jesus (I Peter 5:7)

I AM–Strong in the Lord and in the Power of His Might (Ephesians 6:10)

I AM–Doing All Things through Christ Who Strengthens Me (Philippians 4:13)

I AM–An Heir of God and a Joint Heir with Jesus (Romans 8:17)

I AM–Heir to the Blessings of Abraham (Galatians 3:13, 14)

I AM–Observing and Doing the Lord's Commandments (Deuteronomy 28: 12)

I AM–Blessed Coming in and Blessed Going out (Deuteronomy 28:6)

I AM–An Heir of Eternal Life (I John 5:11, 12)

I AM–Blessed with All Spiritual Blessings (Ephesians 1:3)

I AM–Healed by His Stripes (I Peter 2:24)

I AM–Exercising My Authority over the Enemy (Luke 10:19)

I AM–Above Only and Not Beneath (Deuteronomy 28:13)

I AM–More than a Conqueror (Romans 8:37)

IAM–Establishing God's Word Here on Earth (Matthew 16:19) *I AM*–An Overcomer by the Blood of the Lamb and the Word of My Testimony (Revelation 12:11)

I AM–Daily overcoming the Devil (I John 4:4)

I AM–Not Moved by What I See (II Corinthians 4:18)

IAM–Walking by Faith and Not by Sight (II Corinthians 5:7)

IAM–Casting Down Vain Imaginations (II Corinthians 10:4, 5)

I AM–Bringing Every Thought into Captivity (II Corinthians 10:5)

I AM–Being Transformed by Renewing My Mind (Romans 12:1, 2)

I AM–Reigning in Life through Christ Jesus (Romans 5:17)

IAM–The Righteousness of God in Christ (II Corinthians 5:21)

I AM–An Imitator of Jesus (Ephesians 5:1)

I AM–The Light of the World (Matthew 5:14)

I AM–Blessing the Lord at All Times and Continually Praising the Lord with My Mouth (Psalm 34:1)

Deborah's Resources

The parameters of abuse bring forth a lot of pain but certainly recovery and healing are necessary within one's journey. The following resources are organizations that are readily avail-able for treating such tragedies. I personally needed resources such as these to help me walk through what transpired in my life. Such resources can assist with your next step toward bringing restoration. My main foundation of recovery and healing was and still is based upon having a relationship with the Lord and delving into God's word. The Bible, as I have stated before, has been my mainstay and belief system to overcome these tragedies. However, it took a combined effort of both the dialectical behavior therapy and God's word to make these personal changes in my life. With these organizations, staff members are trained specifically to handle such occurrences. Here is a list of such organizations.

Hotlines and Call Centers

Darkness to Light
1-866-FOR-LIGHT (866-367-5444)

Darkness to Light offers local information and resources about sexual abuse. You can also text 'LIGHT' to 741741 for crisis support with a trained counselor. These services are 24/7, free of charge, confidential, and will be answered by a trained information and referral representative. Helpline availability varies according to state and call center. Darkness to Light also has resources for reporting child sex abuse and human trafficking.

RAINN 800.656.HOPE (4673)

RAINN, the Rape, Abuse, & Incest National Network, is the nation's largest anti-sexual violence organization and operates the National Sexual Assault Hotline, which is free, confidential, and available 24/7/365 in English and Spanish. RAINN works in partnership with more than 1,000 local sexual assault ser-vice providers across the country and operates the DoD Safe Helpline for the Department of Defense.

RAINN also carries out programs to prevent sexual violence, help survivors, and help bring perpetrators to justice. You can call RAINN for guidance and resources in crisis (though call 911 if it's an emergency), after recent sexual trauma, or to talk about sexual trauma that happened long ago. They can help you find support groups, group therapy, individual counselors, legal aid, emergency shelter, medical attention/accompaniment, crime victim assistance advocacy, and a number of other services in your area. You can also chat online with a counselor at hotline. rainn.org.

Safe Horizon
1-800-621-HOPE (4673)

Safe Horizon has a free, 24/7/365, confidential national hotline in English and Spanish for domestic violence survivors; rape, incest, abuse, and sexual assault survivors; and victims of other violent crimes. Counselors are available to talk about your situation (whether it's recent or not), as well as help you figure out the next steps, whether that's in the form of counseling, legal aid, safety planning, or finding a shelter. They can also help you find in-person counseling, group therapy, legal aid, and other resources, and if you are based in New York, you can receive in-person services at their offices in Brooklyn and Harlem, by appointment.

National Sexual Assault Hotline
1 800 656 HOPE (4673)
Southern Crescent Sexual Assault
& Child Advocacy Center
24-hour Crisis Line 770 477 2177

Shelters, Counseling, and Support Resources

Abused Deaf Women's Services

The Abused Deaf Women's Services (ADWAS) community links page offers a good list of services and centers all over the country to help deaf and/or deaf-blind people who have experienced abuse, as well as information about domestic violence, abuse, and recovery, as well as inspiring survivor stories.

ADWAS is based in Seattle, Washington, and if you're a local, you can attend the center for all kinds of services, including short-term crisis counseling, ongoing individual/family therapy related to domestic violence and sexual assault, group counseling related to childhood sexual assault and domestic violence, psychosocial assessments and evaluation of sexual abuse of children, client advocacy and referrals. They also have a local crisis video call hotline, 24/7/365, which you can reach at 1-(206) 812-1001 or via email at hotline@adwas.org.

Association for Behavioral and Cognitive Therapies

You can search for a qualified cognitive behavioral therapy (CBT) provider, an evidence-based method for treating PTSD, using their search engine, which can help you find someone in your area. The website also has great information on these therapeutic approaches, so you can learn more about treatments that might appeal to you.

Life Healing Center- counseling services of Sarah Tate 678-344-8268 Location near Snellville, Ga. Ms. Tate deals specifically with sexual abuse clients.

Domestic Shelters

Domestic Shelters may be the most comprehensive database for folks seeking shelter from domestic violence. They've verified information on shelters and domestic violence programs across the country. This free service can help if you or a friend is suffering from physical, emotional, psychological, or verbal abuse. They can help you find domestic violence programs based on your location, service, and language needs.

Other services include "24-hour hotlines, service listings, and helpful articles on domestic violence statistics, signs and cycles of abuse, housing services, emergency services, legal and financial services, support groups for women, children and families, and more."

National Center for PTSD

This is a web resource with excellent information on PTSD, including the most effective treatments and what they entail. Although it's geared toward veterans, you don't need to be a vet to use it.

National Organization of Sisters of Color Ending Sexual Assault

SCESA has an excellent resources page for women of color looking for treatment centers and organizations dedicated to serving sexual assault survivors near them. The site also offers music, film, and book recommendations. SCESA is an advocacy organization working on policy change, collaboration with other social justice movements, community awareness, and a number of other advocacy tactics.

Psychology Today

You can use the Psychology Today support group search to find sexual trauma support group therapy near you.

Tiwahe Glu Kini Pi

This is a mental, emotional, and spiritual health resource center for the Lakota nation, particularly for men, women, and children who have experienced trauma. They offer several different programs and services in service of Lakota traditions and wellness.

They offer a range of information for survivors of sexual violence related to understanding how the holistic healing arts can facilitate healing. They also have a helpful list of emergency resources available both over the phone and online, as well as recommended organizations and books for those pursuing alternative healing arts to complement their trauma recovery. These resources also benefit those who support survivors, whether as friends and family, or as healing arts practitioners.

Somatic Therapies

Somatic Experiencing Trauma Institute

This site is a great resource for evidence-based studies about how trauma affects the brain and body, and for information on somatic (body-centered) therapy approaches to recovery. You can also use their directory to find somatic therapists specializing in trauma recovery.

Survivor Art and Art Therapy Sites

Art Therapy Blog

Art Therapy Blog is full of articles and resources for art therapy for adults and children, and specialized projects and research for a number of audiences, ranging from trauma to autism. If you're interested in research and projects, you can try these yourself or with a counselor, therapist, or group.

Last Battle

Founded by Mary Ellen Mann, author of *From Pain to Power: Overcoming Sexual Trauma and Reclaiming Your True Identity*, Last Battle is a creative space for sexual trauma survivors to share their artwork, stories, and poems in the site's gallery.

There is also a blog for inspiration and recovery, Mann's key-note speeches and talks, and a page of "ideas for living well" filled with advice for advocacy, recovery, and support. The site has a Christian slant and uses the metaphor of the princess warrior to explore recovery, and includes exercises and articles on meditation and women's empowerment.

Online Chat and Online Peer Support

1in6

1in6 is a resource for men who have experienced unwanted or abusive sexual experiences. They offer recovery information for men, men's stories of trauma and recovery, 24/7/365 online chat support with trained advocates through their website, and anonymous online support groups facilitated by a professional counselor. Support groups meet every Monday and Wednesday.

Male Survivor

Male Survivor is a collection of resources and articles for men who have experienced sexual trauma, as well as a forum for men to discuss trauma and recovery. Resources include a therapist directory to help find therapists who specialize in treating male survivors of sexual trauma; a support group directory; peer support guide; male survivor forum; resources directory; healing events; and the Hope Healing Support Team, who are available by email to answer any questions survivors may have.

National Sexual Violence Resource Center

The NSVRC offers up-to-date research and resources on sexual-violence recovery, including news, projects, special collections, publications, and a library. They also offer a very helpful database for survivors seeking help in the form of individual or group counseling, support groups, community outreach, advocacy, and more.

"NSVRC enjoys a strong partnership with state, territorial, and tribal anti-sexual assault coalitions and national allied organizations. This online directory highlights those organizations and projects working to eliminate sexual violence." You can search by state to help find resources near you.

Protect Our Defenders

Protect Our Defenders (POD) is the only national organization solely dedicated to ending the epidemic of rape and sexual assault in the military and to combating a culture of pervasive misogyny, sexual harassment, and retribution against victims.

POD supports survivors of military sexual assault and sexual harassment, including service members, veterans, and civilians assaulted by members of the military. Resources include hotlines you can call, applications for free legal services, directories for local services, peer-to-peer support, resource libraries, and forums.

Survivorship: for survivors of ritual abuse, mind-control, and torture

This resource is not a replacement for therapy, but rather an online space for survivors of a very specific kind of sexual abuse or trauma to share and validate their experiences with each other as peers.

Survivorship has yearly conferences and video resources, and for membership access, which costs "$75 down to what you think you can pay," which will provide you with updates every other month with news of the organization, national events, and news articles for survivors. Two times per year, you will receive their journal, which contains many articles, poems, and artwork by survivors, therapists, family or friends of survivors, and other supporters. You will also be able to use the members-only section of the website.

Survivors Network of those Abused by Priests

SNAP is dedicated to supporting survivors who have been abused by priests or other religious figures like nuns, religion teachers, or ministers. The organization is run by volunteers who help survivors find therapists specializing in religious abuse and sexual abuse in their area, as well as assistance in reporting abusers and finding legal aid.

SNAP also has a number of group therapy chapters, and you can use their directory to find one near you. They also have annual conferences for you to check out and a collection of survivors' stories and related news.

Retreats

Break the Silence Against Domestic Violence (BTS)

BTS offers an Annual Survivor Sister Retreat for women who are affected by domestic violence. The retreat is an opportunity to immerse yourself in activities, workshops, and classes focused on holistic approaches to healing, as well as to forge friendships and supportive relationships with other survivors.

This retreat best suits women who are not currently in an unhealthy relationship or suicidal. BTS suggests seeking crisis help first, and then attending the retreat when you are in a more stable place to begin a lifelong journey of loving aware-ness and healing.

<u>The Refuge: A Healing Place</u>

The Refuge offers a Rape-Related Trauma Treatment and Rehab Center for rape and sexual assault survivors. This residential treatment center, located in Florida, offers several therapeutic approaches to healing sexual trauma, including exposure therapy (specifically, recalling painful memories in a safe environment with a professional), interpersonal therapy, cognitive behavioral therapy, mindfulness-based cognitive therapy, and intensive family therapy.

Experiential therapy is also a large part of their approach and can include dramatic experiencing, hypnosis, art therapy, a ropes course, equine therapy, creative expression, group sharing, music therapy, and journaling. The Refuge is sur-rounded by beautiful nature, and in their spare time, clients are welcome to play sports, fish, hike, and enjoy the grounds.

Deborah's Bookshelf

Steve Arterburn: *Healing Is a Choice*
Robert McGee: *The Search for Significance*
Joyce Meyer: *Battlefield of the Mind*
Joyce Meyer: *Beauty for Ashes*
R.T. Kendall: *How to Forgive Ourselves—Totally*
Sandra D. Wilson: *Into Abba's Arms*
David G. Benner: *The Gift of Being Yourself*
David G. Benner: *Healing Emotional Wounds*
Beth Moore: *Audacious*
Beth Moore: *Believing God*
Beth Moore: *When Godly People Do Ungodly Things*
John Bradshaw: *Healing Shame That Binds You*
Eliana Gil, Ph.D.: *Outgrowing the Pain*
Charles Stanley: *The Source of My Strength*
Elizabeth George: *Loving God with All Your Mind*
Diane Mandt Langberg, Ph.D.: *On the Threshold of Hope*
Perry Noble: *Unleash!*
Bruce Wilkinson: *The Prayer of Jabez*
Harriet Goldhor Lerner, Ph.D.: *The Dance of Anger*
A.W. Tozer: *The Pursuit of God*
Max Lucado: *In the Grip of Grace*

John Eldredge: *Waking the Dead*

Jerry Bridges: Who Am I?

Elyse M Fitzpatrick: Comforts from The Cross

Nancy DeMoss Wolgemuth: Lies Women Believe

Sandi Patty: The Voice

Christopher Ash: Out of the Storm: Grappling with God in the Book of Job

Elyse M. Fitzpatrick: Found in Him: The joy of the Incarnation and our union with Christ

Jerry Bridges, Robert Bevington: The Great Exchange

Jerry Bridges: The Gospel for Real Life: Turn to the Liberating Power of the Cross

Elyse M. Fitzpatrick: Because He Loves Me

Matt Chandler: Recovering Redemption

C.J. Mahaney: How Can I Change?

Greg Gilbert: What is the Gospel?

Charles Leiter: Justification and Regeneration

Jerry Bridges: Trusting God

Jim Berg: Essential Virtues: Marks of the Christ-Centered Life

Walter Marshall, Bruce McRae: The Gospel Mystery of Sanctification

Jim Berg: Changed Into His Image

Jim Berg: Christ Formed in You: The Power of eh Gospel for Personal Change

Jim Berg: Created for His Glory

Brad Bigney: Gospel Treason

Steve Gallagher: At the Alter of Sexual Idolatry

Elyse Fitzpatrick: Idols of the Heart

Notes

About the Author

Deborah White resides in McDonough, Georgia with her husband, Marshall. She happily attends church in Griffin, Georgia, where acceptance and love are freely given. Attending her Lifegroup is one of her favorite places to learn about God's unconditional love and grace. She has four children, one being in heaven, and four grandchildren that she loves being with. She daily enjoys taking new steps on her journey of learning to rest in the arms of her Abba, Father, God.

www.ingramcontent.com/pod-product-compliance
Lightning Source LLC
Chambersburg PA
CBHW060528130626
46553CB00002B/684